BIG-NOTE PIANO

Disney

HEROES AND SHEROES

T0086952

ISBN 978-1-70515-501-1

Visit Hal Leonard Online at
www.halleonard.com

Contact us:
Hal Leonard
7777 West Bluemound Road
Milwaukee, WI 53213
Email: info@halleonard.com

In Europe, contact:
Hal Leonard Europe Limited
42 Wigmore Street
Marylebone, London, W1U 2RN
Email: info@halleonardeurope.com

In Australia, contact:
Hal Leonard Australia Pty. Ltd.
4 Lentara Court
Cheltenham, Victoria, 3192 Australia
Email: info@halleonard.com.au

CONTENTS

I AM MOANA
(Song of the Ancestors)
from MOANA

Music by LIN-MANUEL MIRANDA,
OPETAIA FOA'I and MARK MANCINA
Lyrics by Lin-Manuel Miranda
and OPETAIA FOA'I

Moderately, with expression

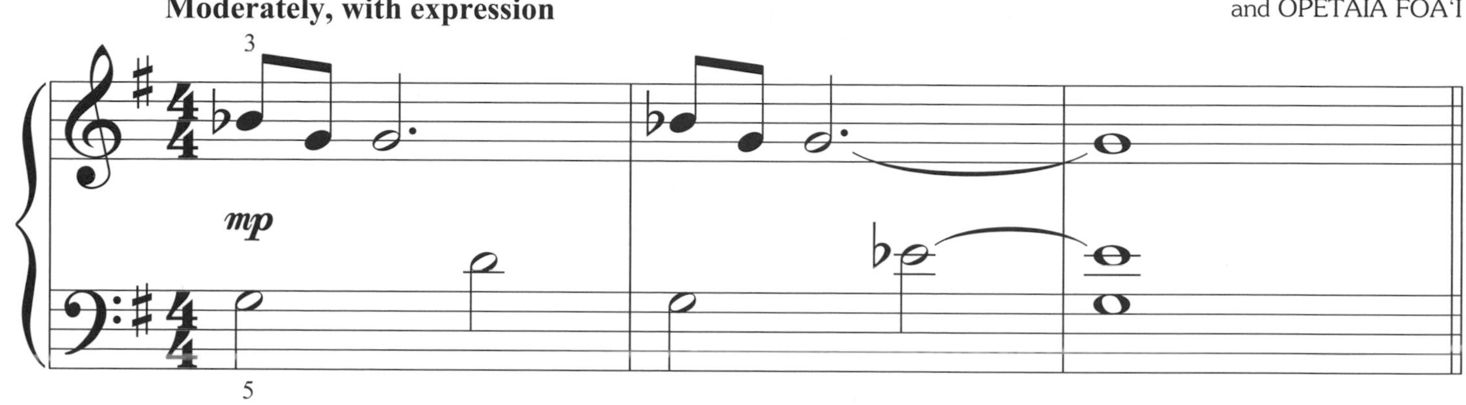

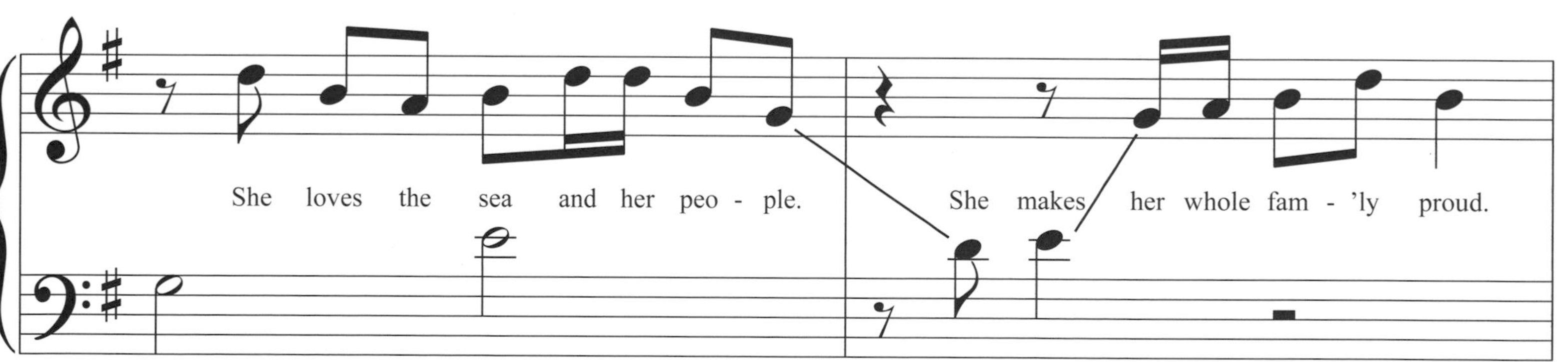

but scars can heal and re - veal just where you are.

The peo - ple you love will change you.
The things you have learned will guide you.

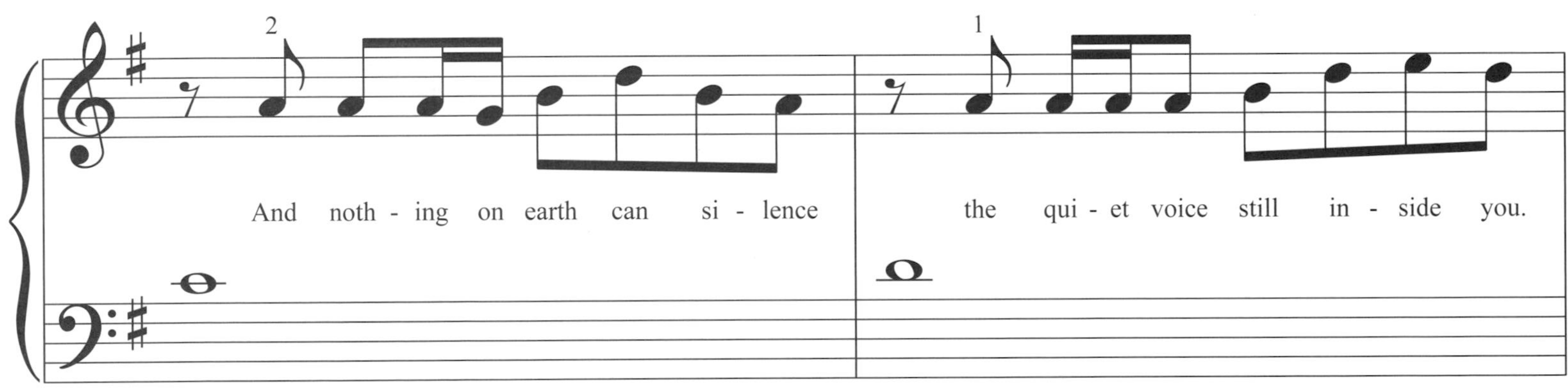
2
1
And noth - ing on earth can si - lence
the qui - et voice still in - side you.

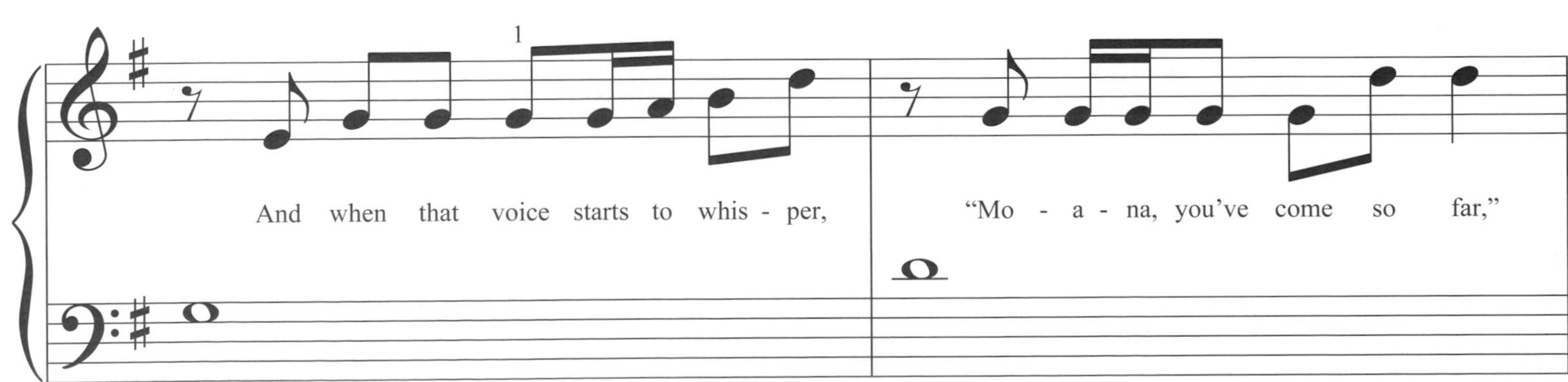
1
And when that voice starts to whis - per,
"Mo - a - na, you've come so far,"

1
4
Mo - a - na, lis - ten: do you know who you are?

MOANA:
3
Who am I?
I am a girl who loves my is - land, and the girl who loves the

2
sea: it calls me. I am the daugh-ter of the vil - lage

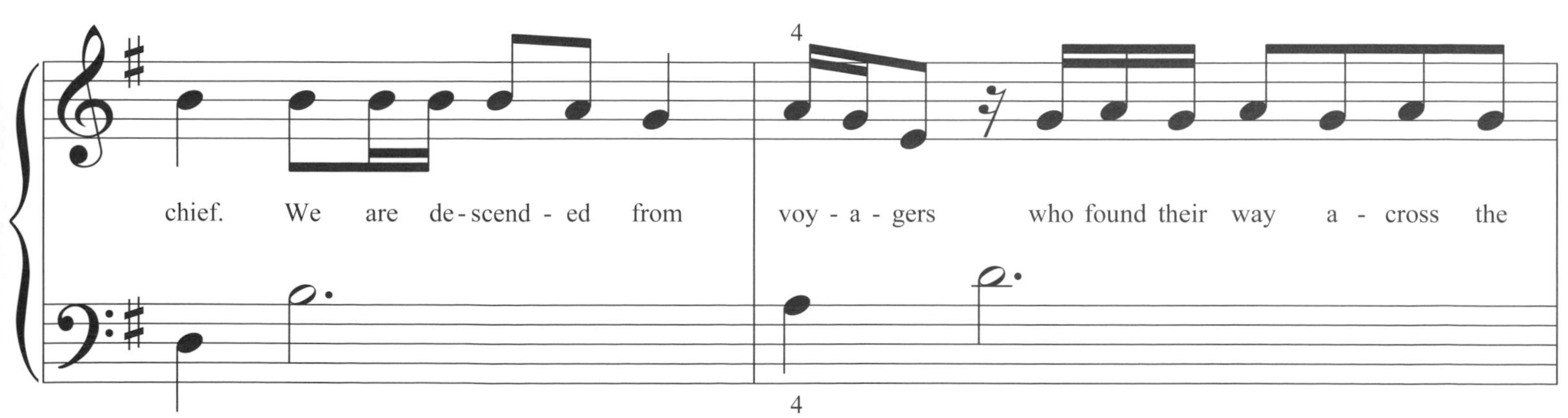
4
chief. We are de - scend - ed from voy - a - gers who found their way a - cross the
4

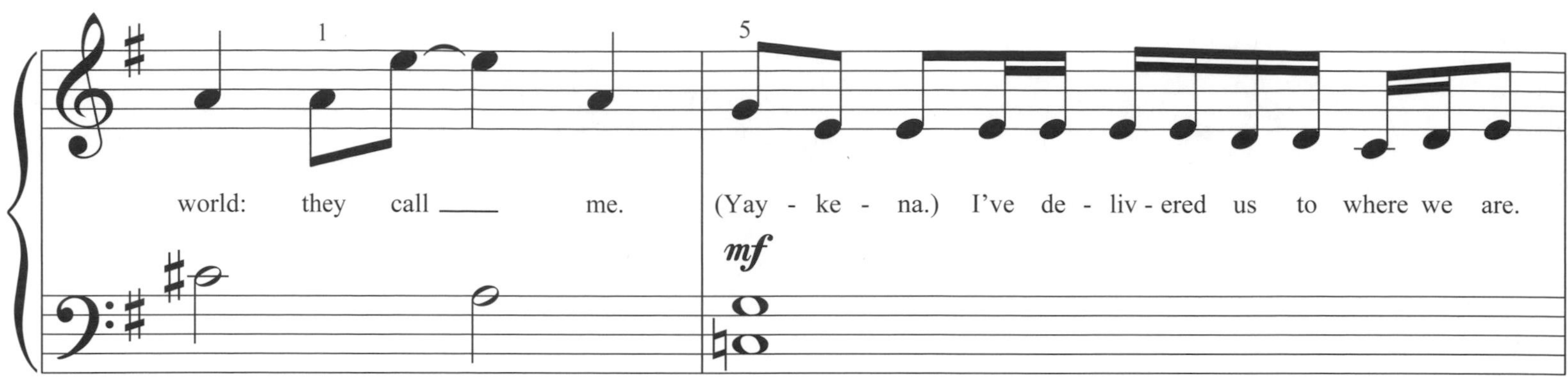
world: they call ___ me.
(Yay - ke - na.) I've de - liv - ered us to where we are.
mf

(Yay - ke - na.) I have jour - neyed far - ther.
(Yay - ke - na.) I am ev - 'ry - thing I've learned and

more. Still it calls me.
And the
rit.
f
call is - n't out there at all, it's in -
a tempo

side me. It's like the
tide, al - ways fall - ing and

ris - ing. I will car - ry you here in my heart; you re -

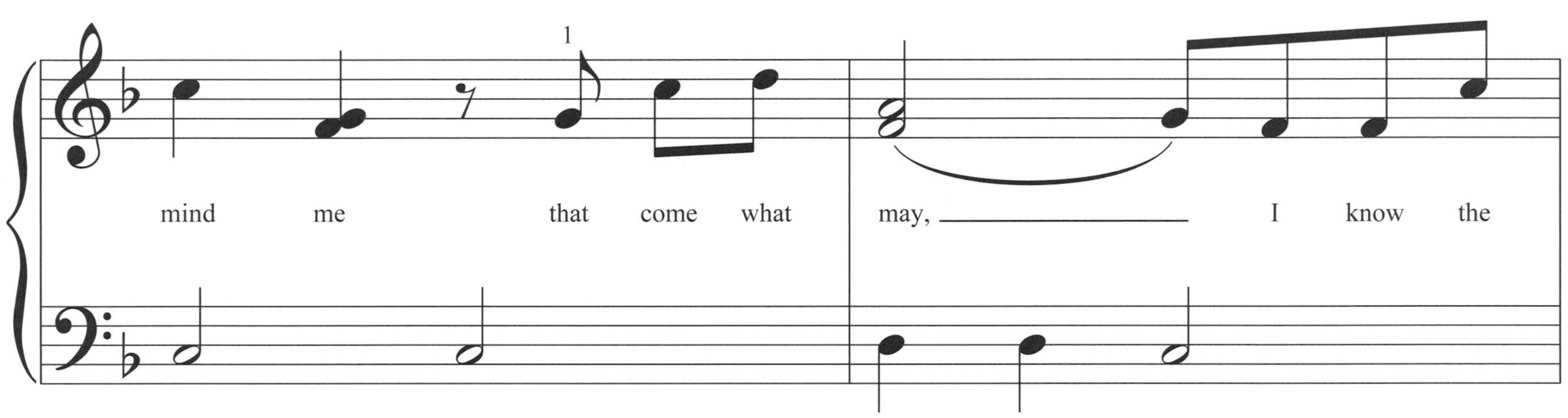
1
mind me that come what may, I know the

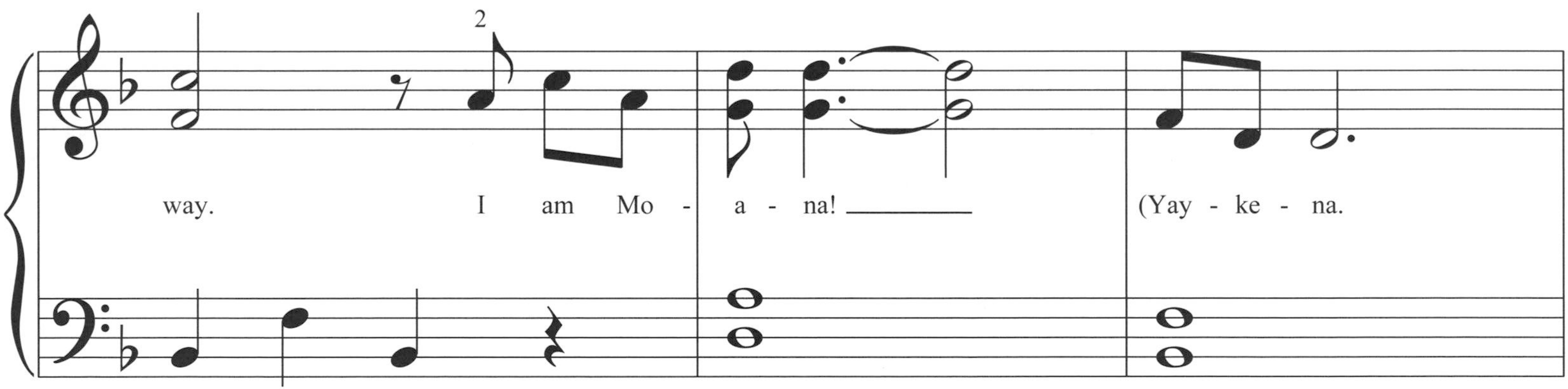
2
way. I am Mo - a - na! (Yay - ke - na.

Yay - ke - na. Yay - ke - na Ta - ma toe te - ney!)

ELASTIGIRL IS BACK

from INCREDIBLES 2

Composed by MICHAEL GIACCHINO

EVERMORE
from BEAUTY AND THE BEAST 2017

Music by ALAN MENKEN
Lyrics by TIM RICE

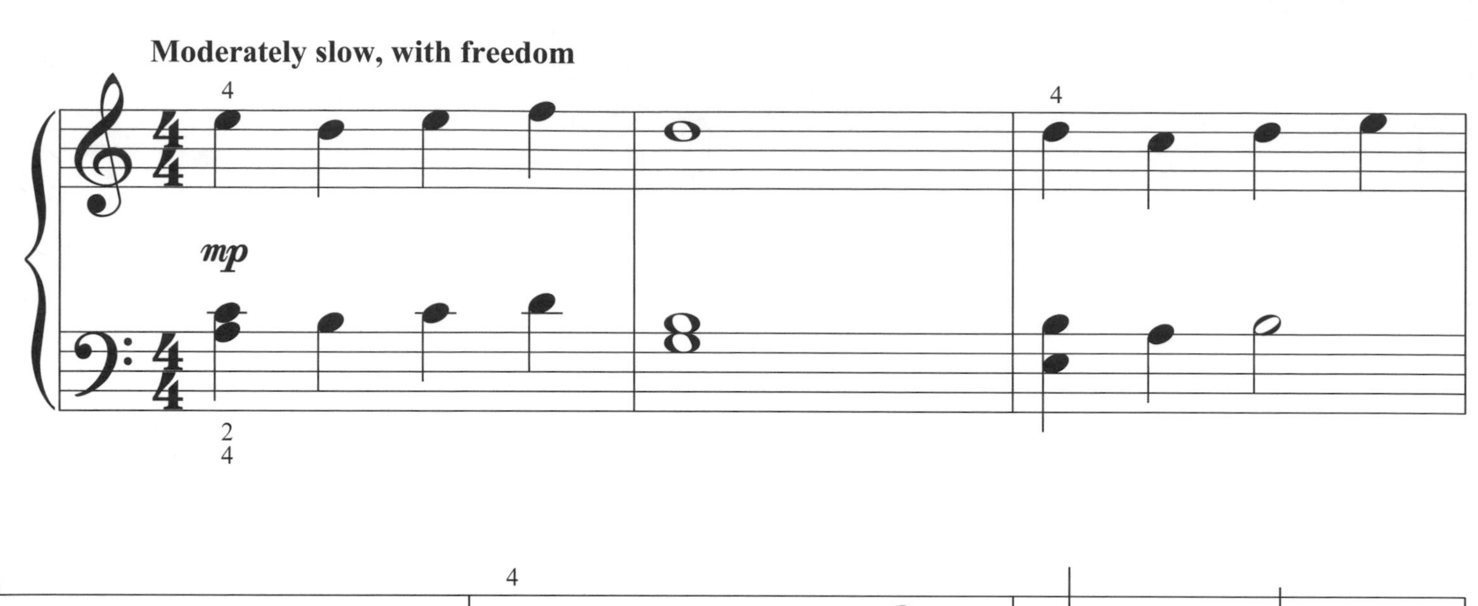

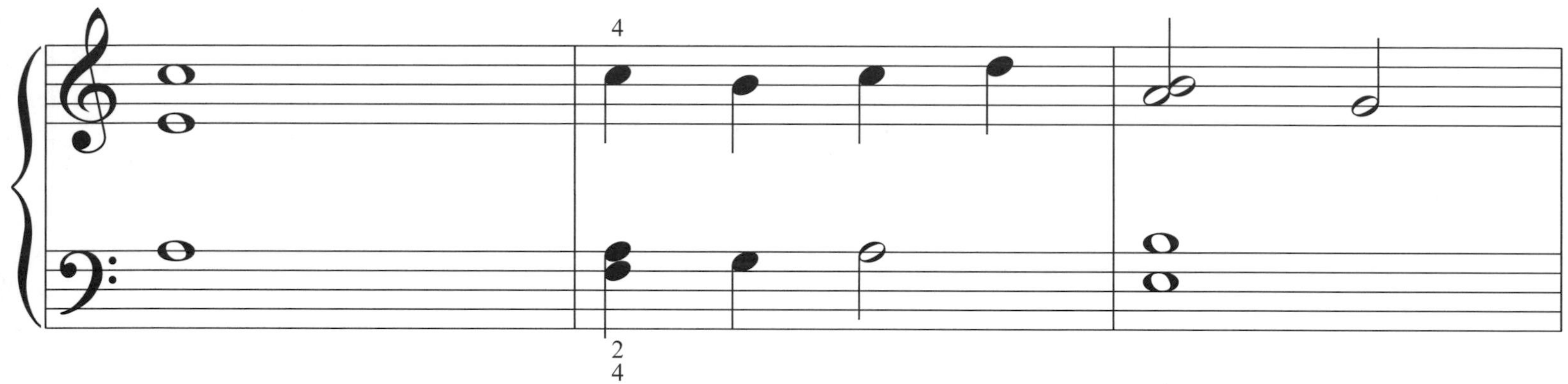

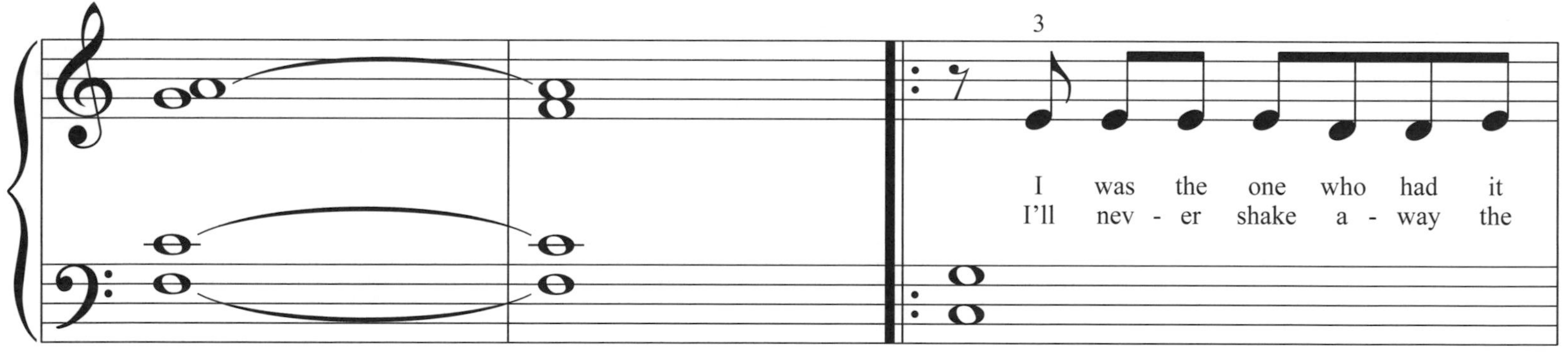

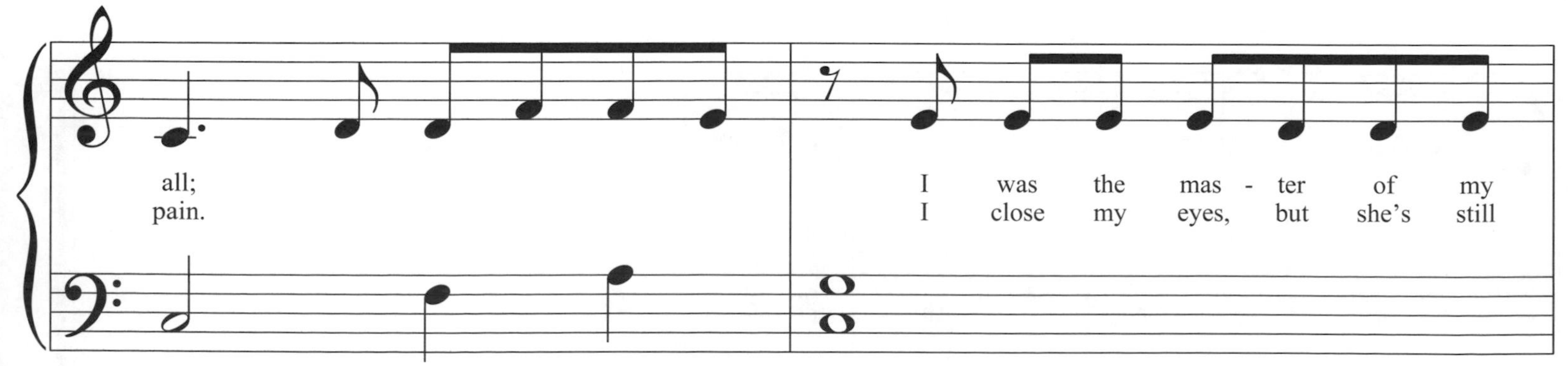

fate.
there.
I nev - er need - ed an - y - bod - y in my life;
I let her steal in - to my mel - an - chol - y heart;
I learned the truth too late.
it's more than I can
1.
2.
bear.
Now I know she'll nev - er leave me, e - ven
mf
as she runs a - way. She will still tor - ment me,

calm me, hurt me, move me, come what may.
Wast - ing in my lone - ly tow - er,
wait - ing by an o - pen door,
I'll fool my - self she'll walk right in,
and be with me for - ev - er - more.
2
3
2 1 2

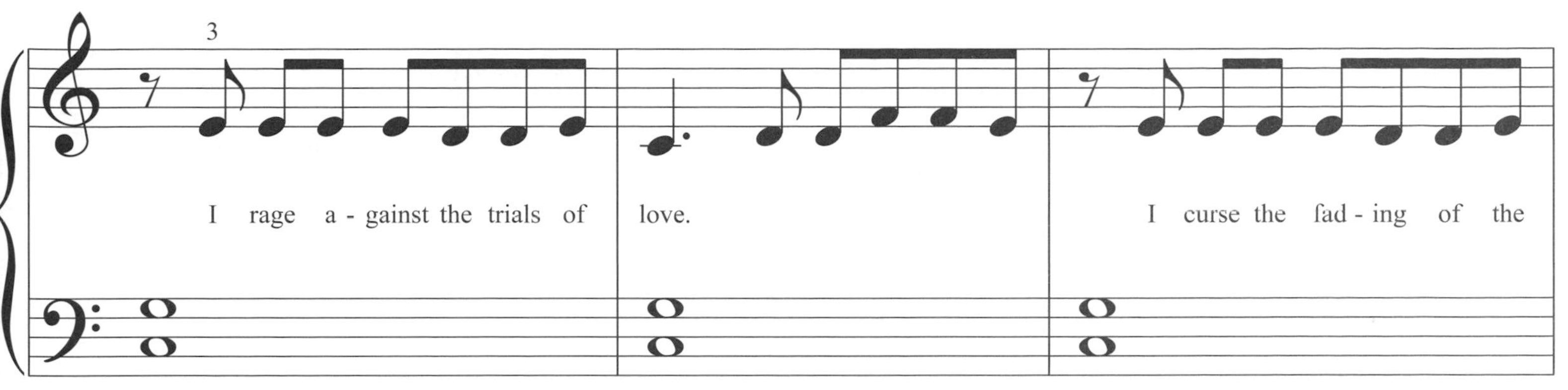
3
I rage a - gainst the trials of
love.
I curse the fad - ing of the

2
light.
2
Though she's al - read - y flown so
far be - yond my reach,

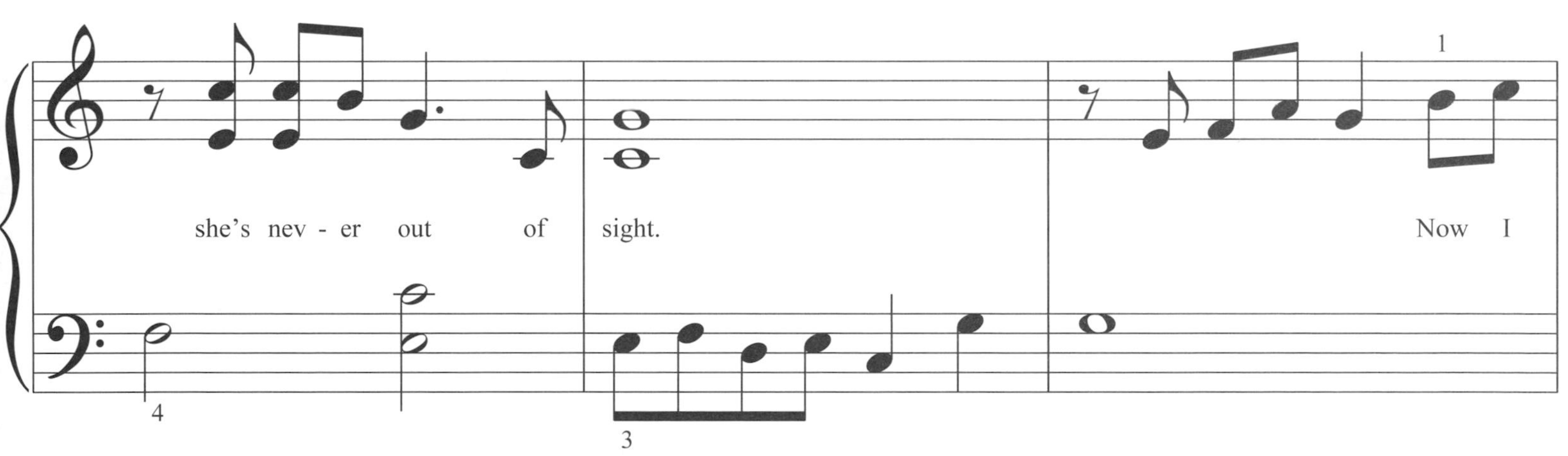
she's nev - er out of
sight.
1
Now I
4
3

know she'll nev - er
1
leave me, e - ven
as she fades from

view. She will still in - spire me, be a part of
3

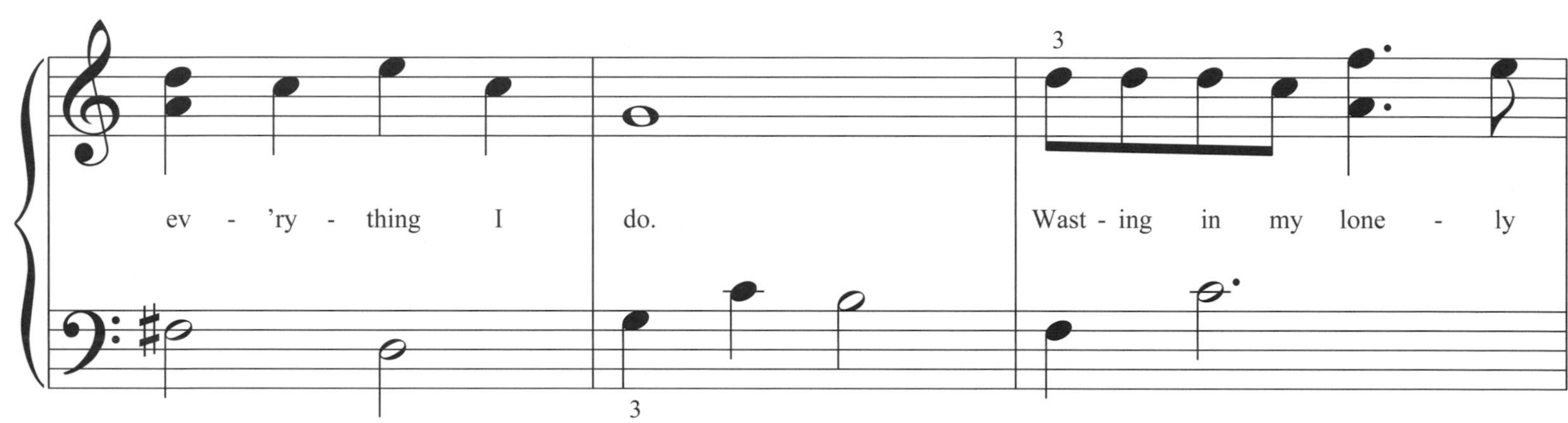
ev - 'ry - thing I do. Wast - ing in my lone - ly
3
3

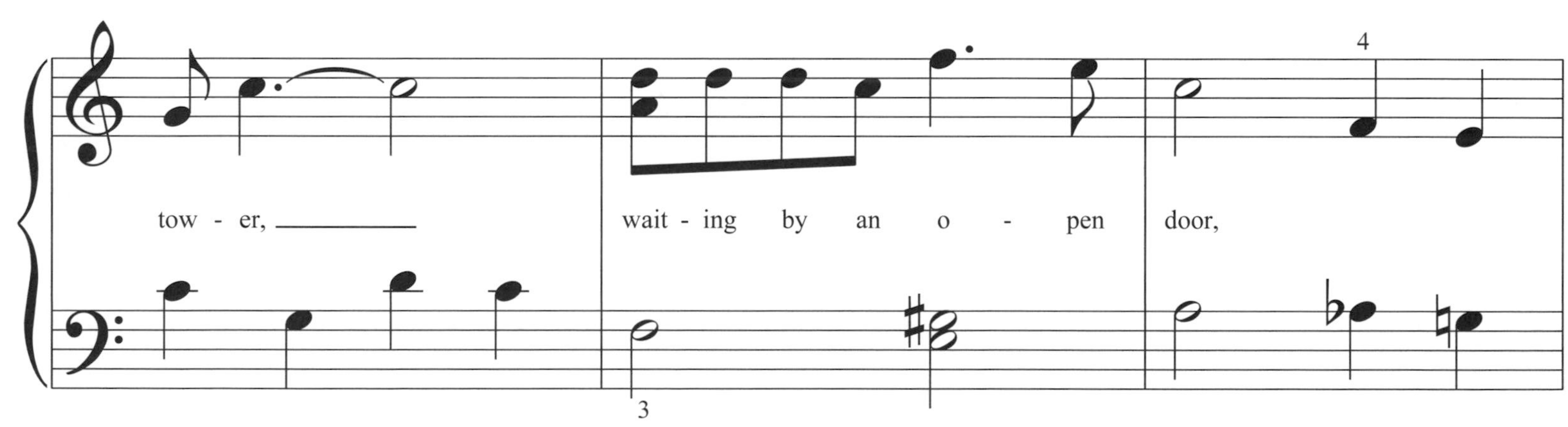
tow - er, wait - ing by an o - pen door,
4
3

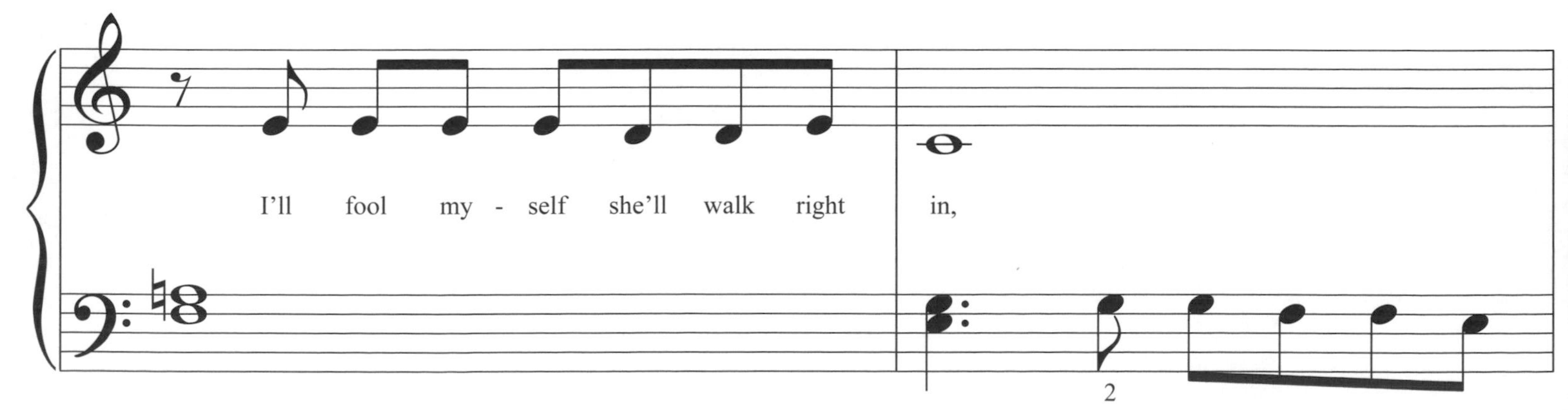
I'll fool my - self she'll walk right in,
2

and as the long, long nights be - gin,

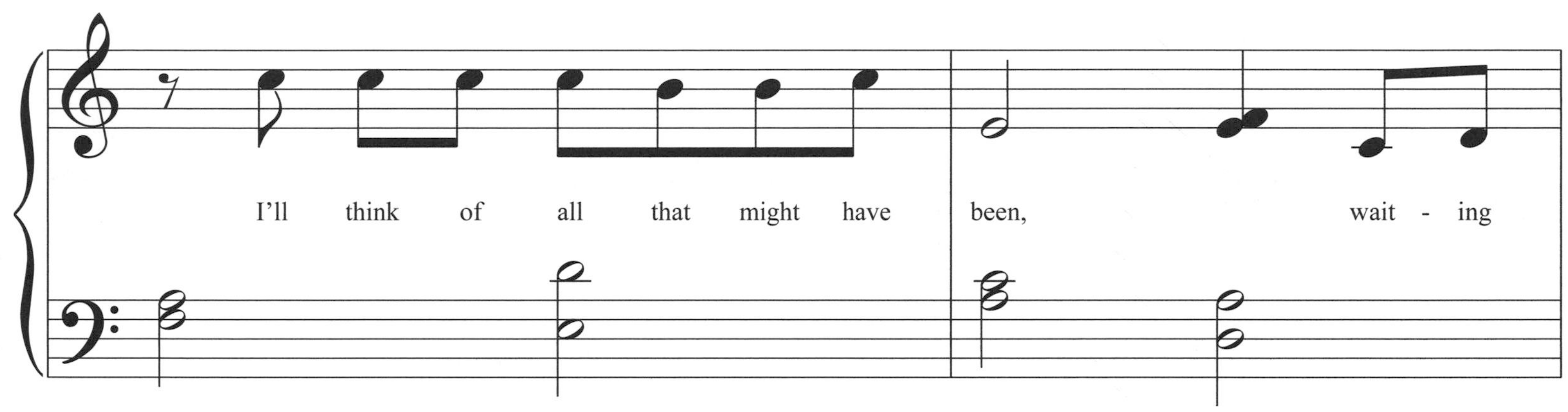
I'll think of all that might have been, wait - ing

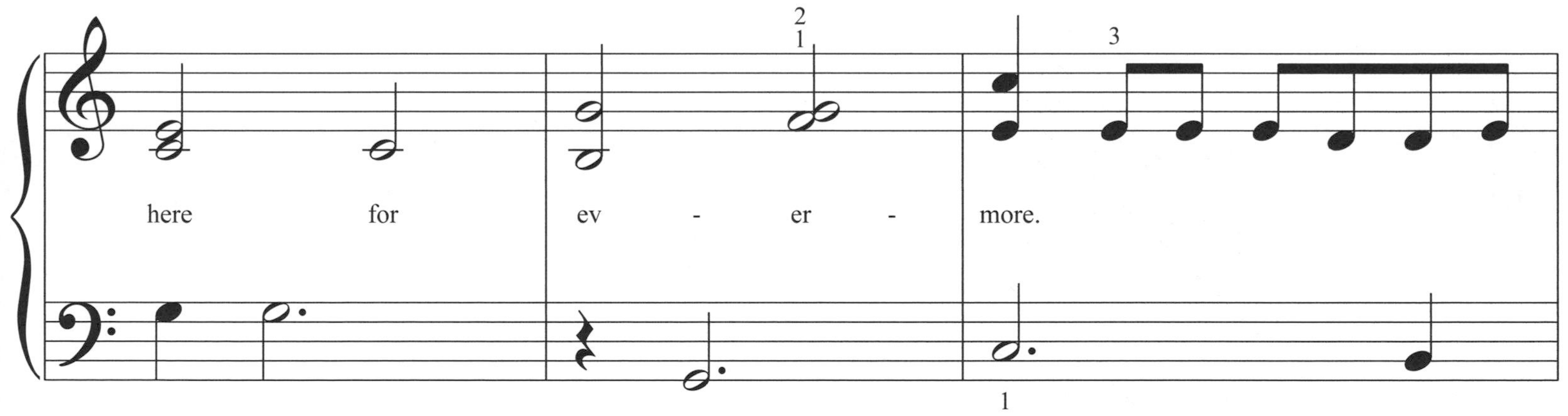
here for ev - er - more.
2
1
3
1

HAWAIIAN ROLLER COASTER RIDE

from LILO & STITCH

Words and Music by ALAN SILVESTRI
and MARK KEALI'I HO'OMALU

Moderately fast

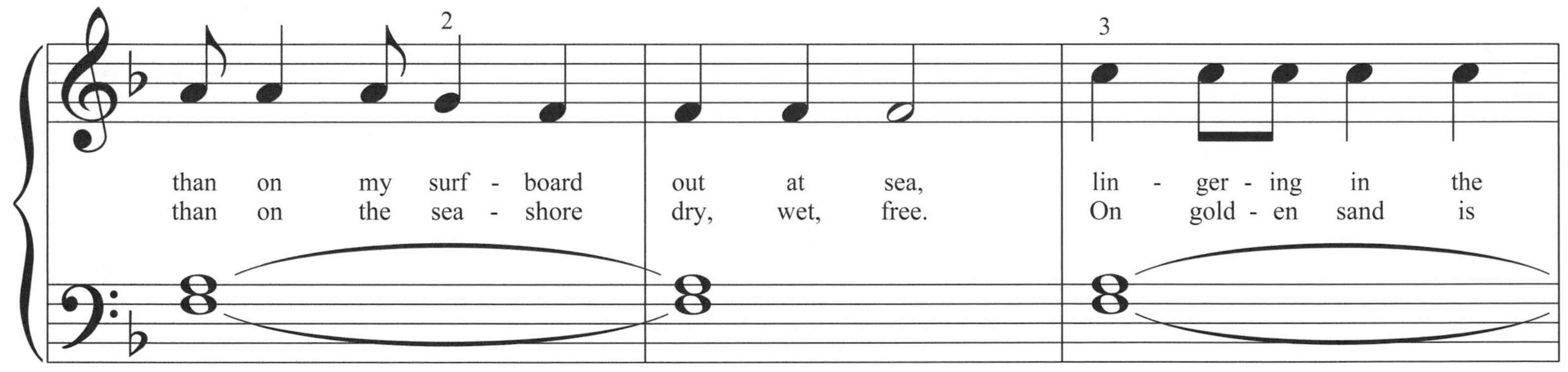

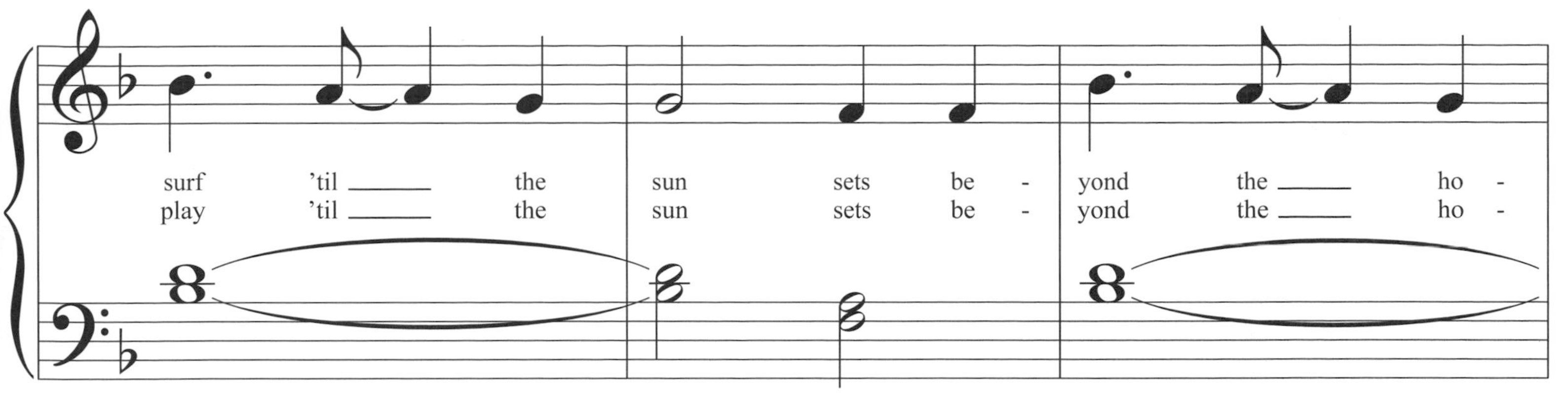
surf 'til the sun sets be - yond the ho -
play 'til the sun sets be - yond the ho -

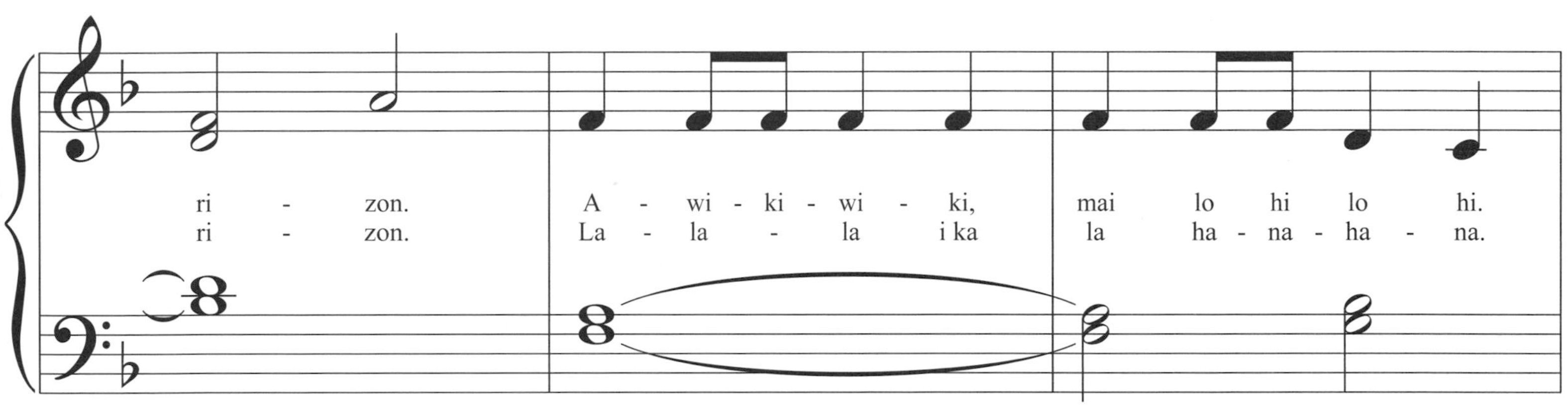
ri - zon. A - wi - ki - wi - ki, mai lo hi lo hi.
ri - zon. La - la - la i ka la ha - na - ha - na.

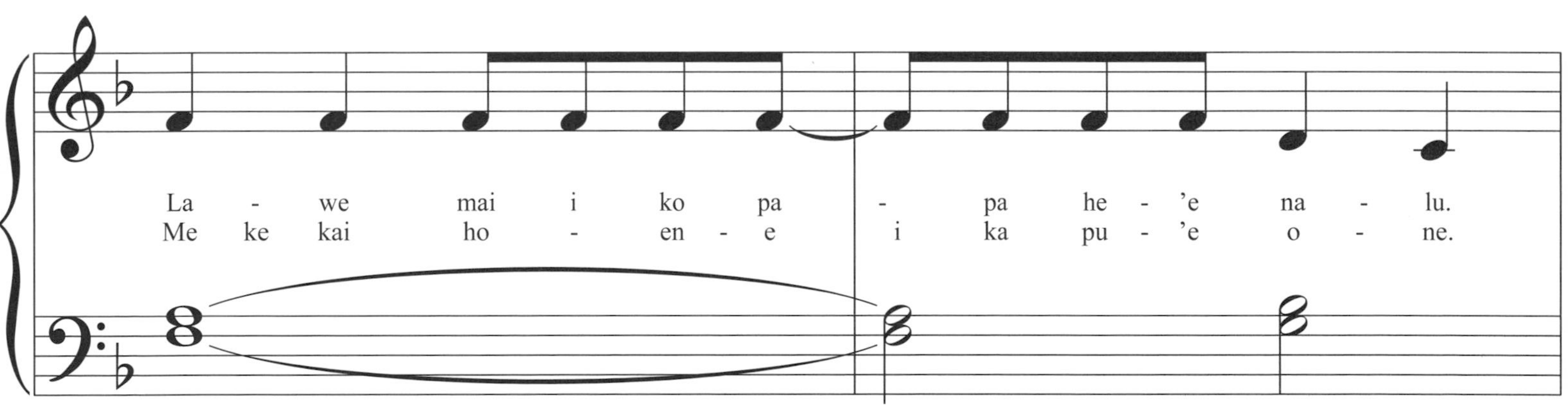
La - we mai i ko pa - pa he - 'e na - lu.
Me ke kai ho - en - e i ka pu - 'e o - ne.

3
1
Fly - ing by on a Ha - wai - ian roll - er
It's time to try the Ha - wai - ian roll - er

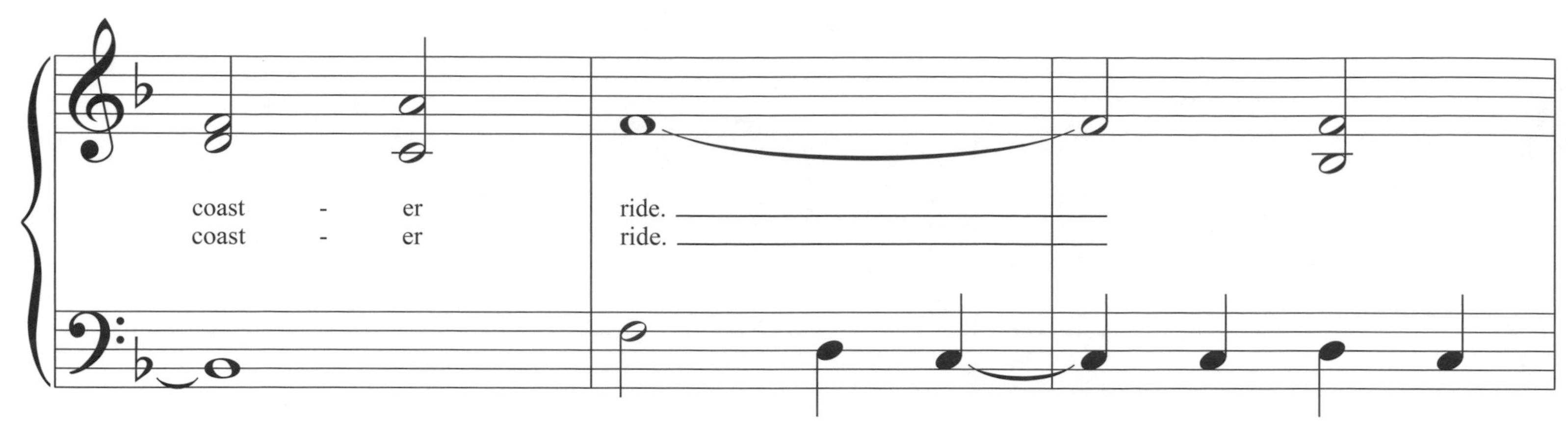
coast - er ride.
coast - er ride.

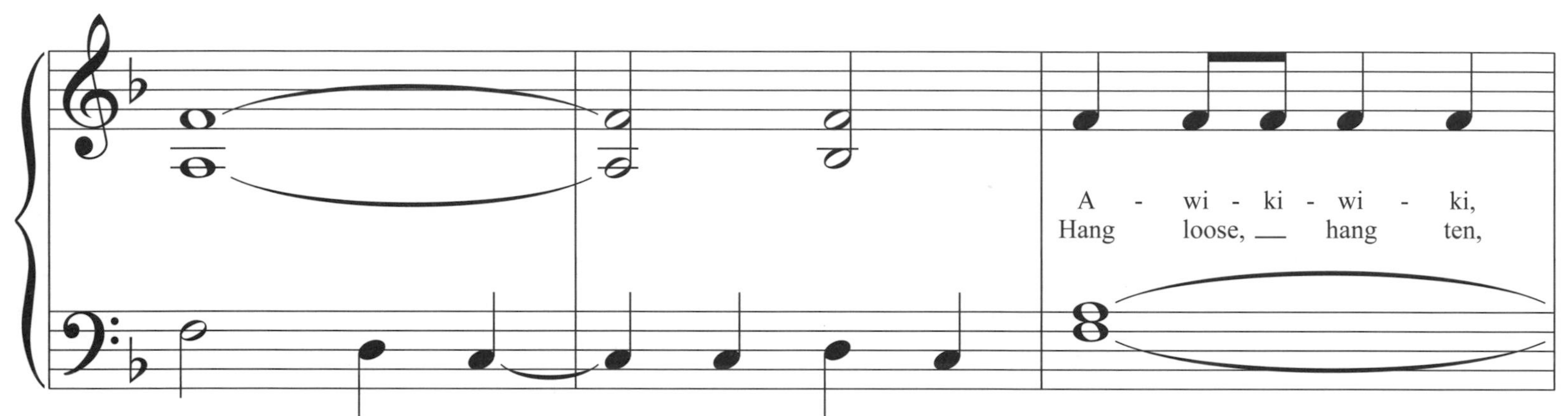
A - wi - ki - wi - ki,
Hang loose, hang ten,

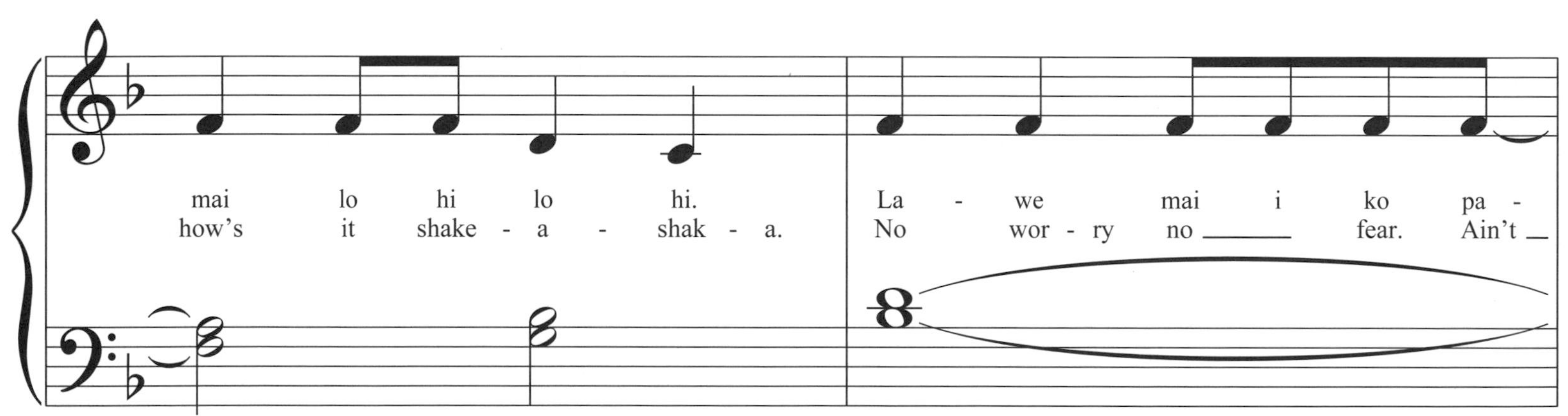
mai lo hi lo hi.
how's it shake - a - shak - a.
La - we mai i ko pa -
No wor - ry no fear. Ain't

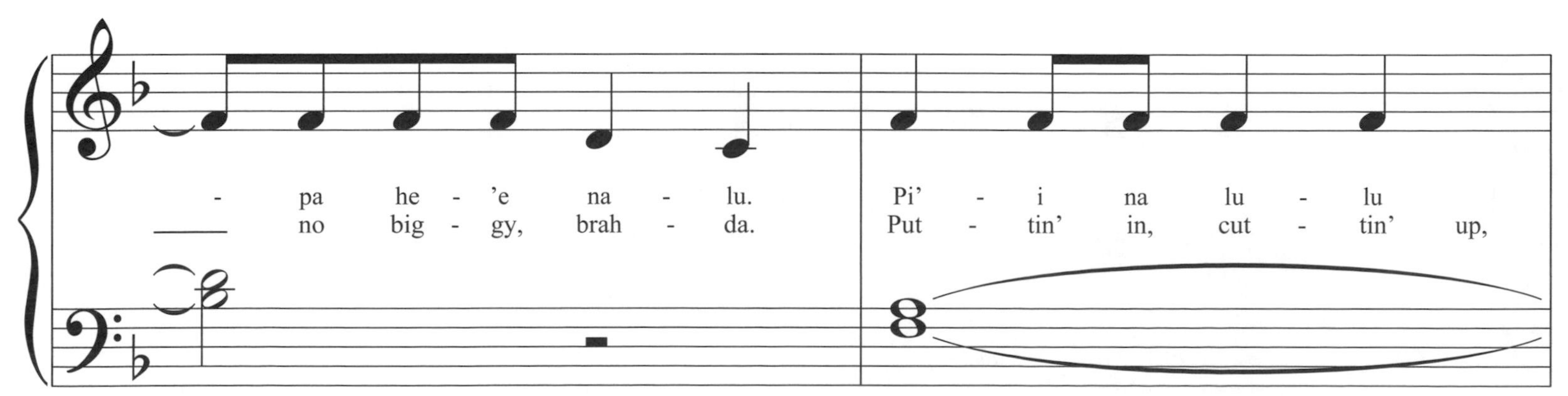
- pa he - 'e na - lu.
no big - gy, brah - da.
Pi' - i na lu - lu
Put - tin' in, cut - tin' up,

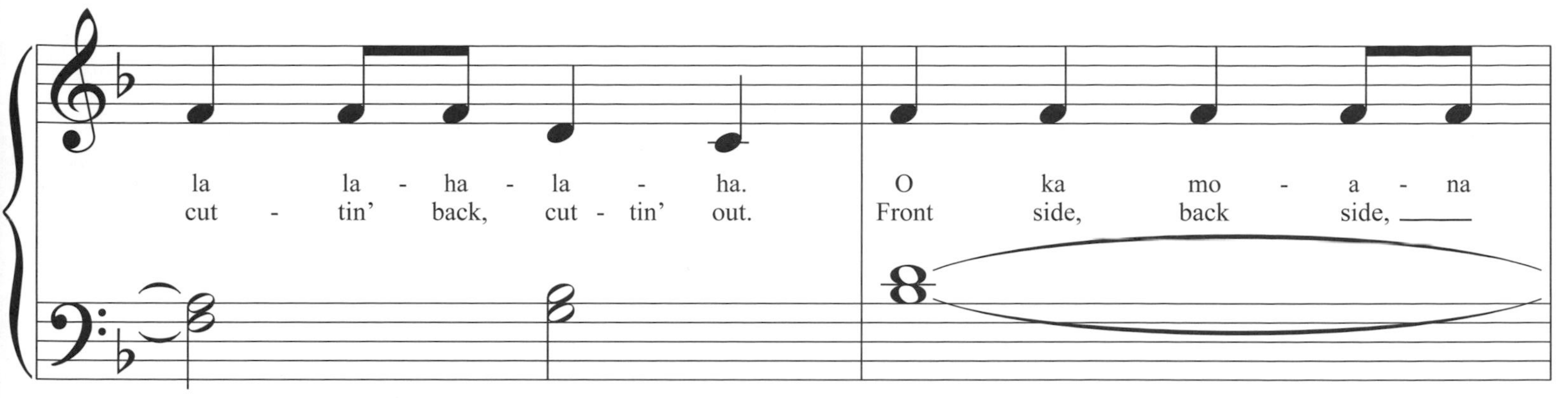
la la - ha - la - ha.
cut - tin' back, cut - tin' out.
O ka mo - a - na
Front side, back side,

To Coda
1.
ha - nu - pa - nu - pa.
goof - y foot - ed wipe out.
La - la - la i ka
la ha - na - ha - na.

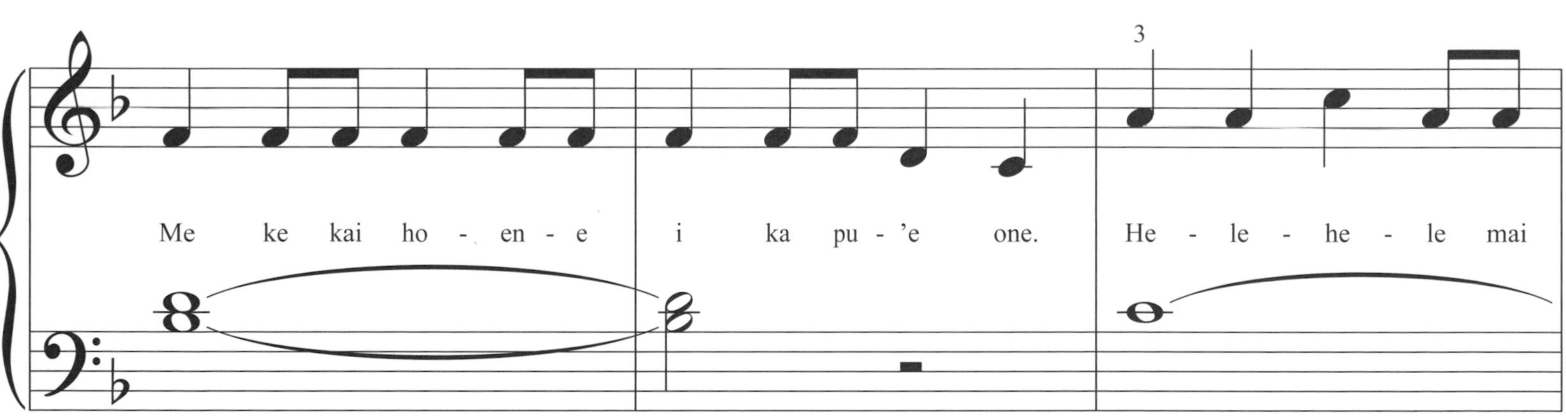
Me ke kai ho - en - e
i ka pu - 'e one.
3
He - le - he - le mai

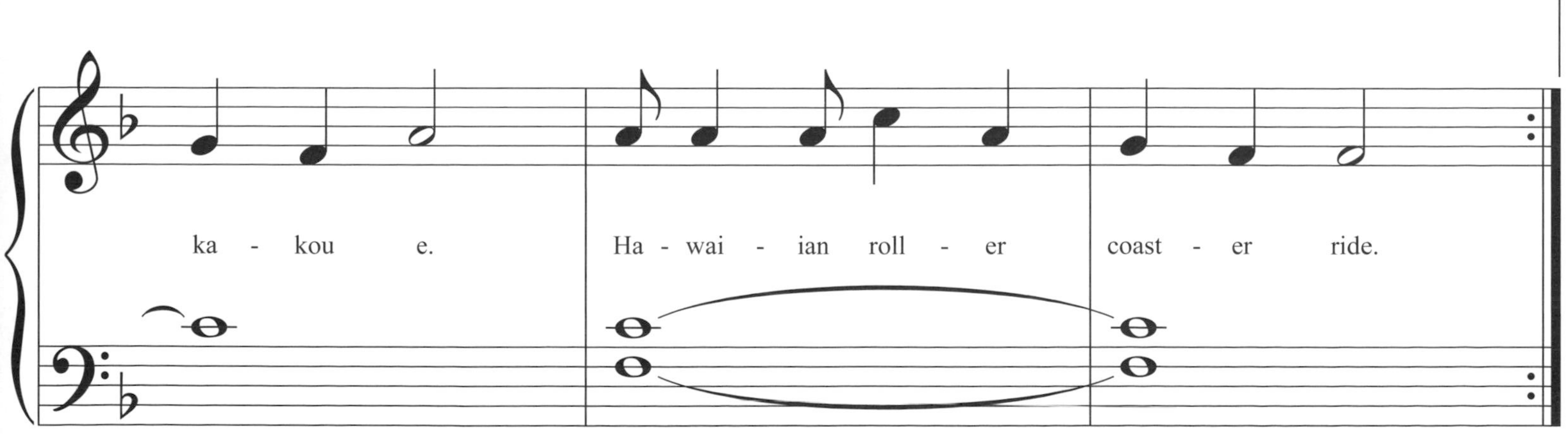
ka - kou e.
Ha - wai - ian roll - er
coast - er ride.

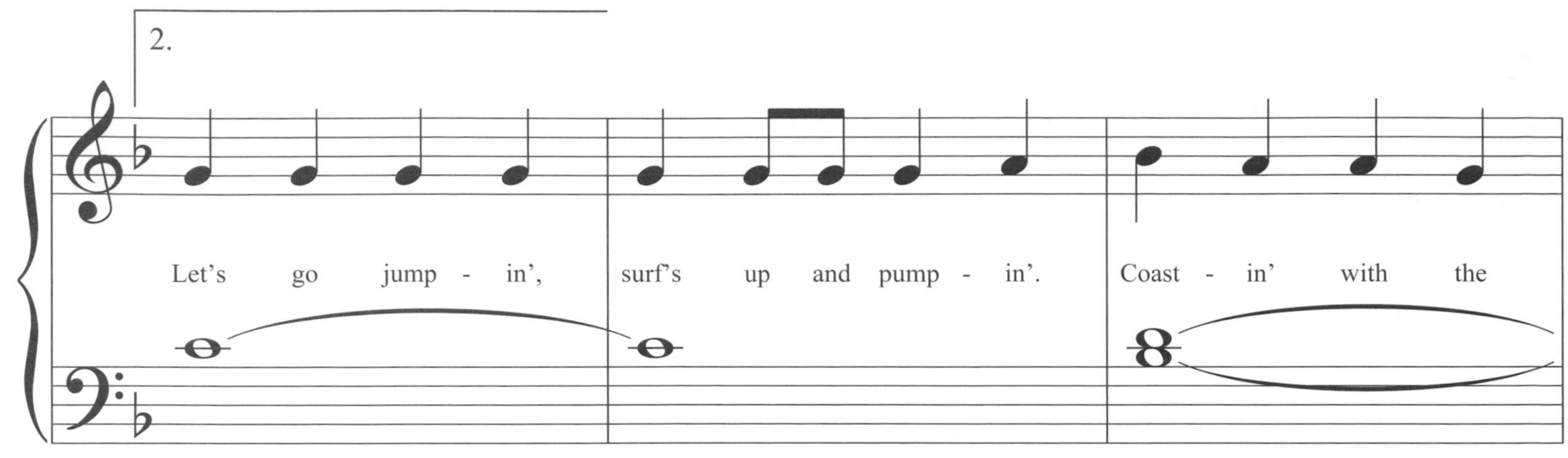
2.
Let's go jump - in', surf's up and pump - in'. Coast - in' with the

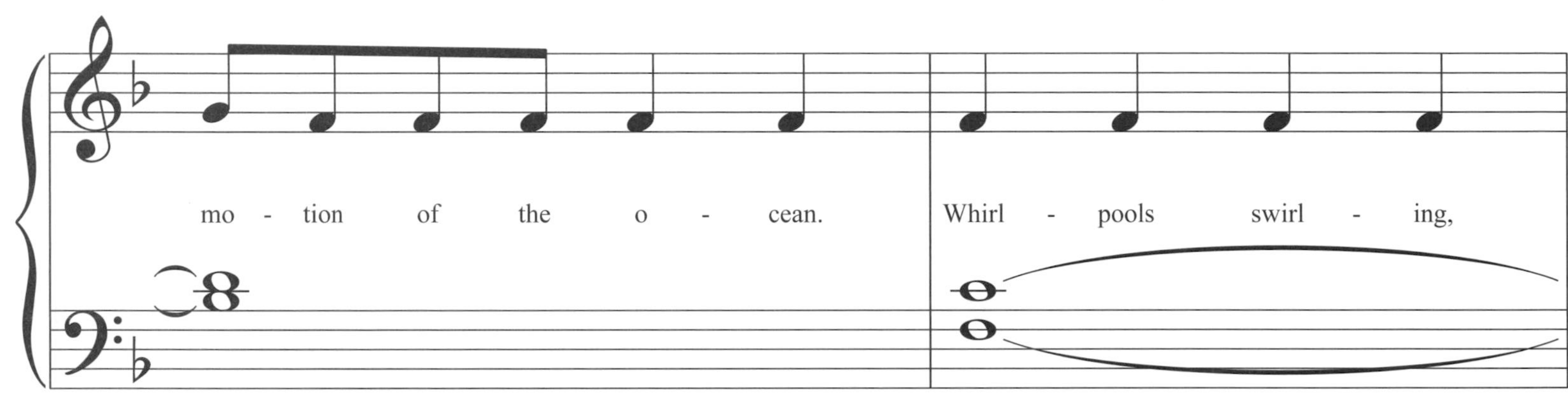
mo - tion of the o - cean. Whirl - pools swirl - ing,

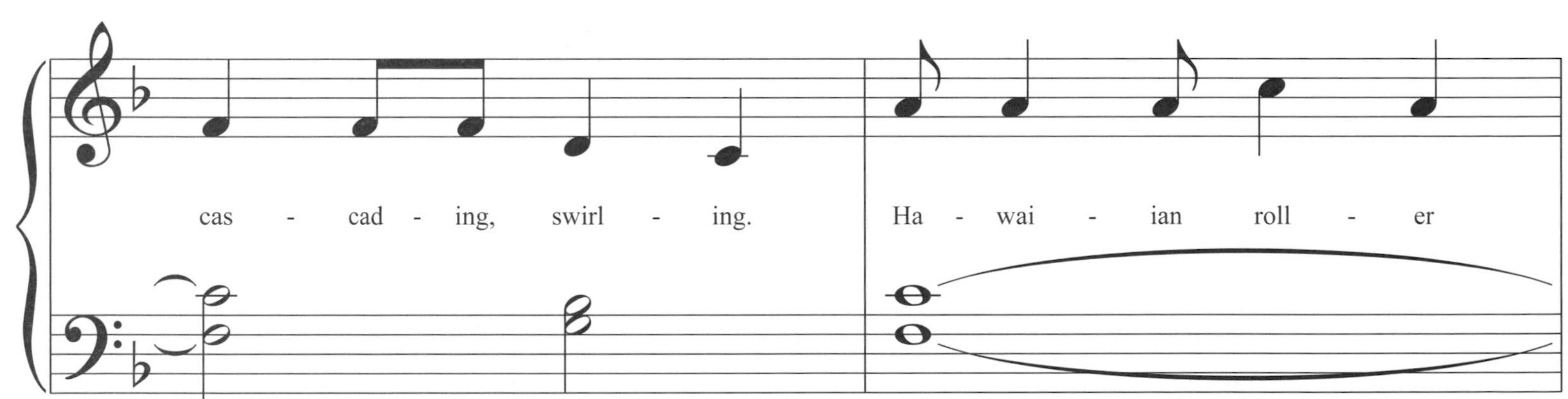
cas - cad - ing, swirl - ing. Ha - wai - ian roll - er

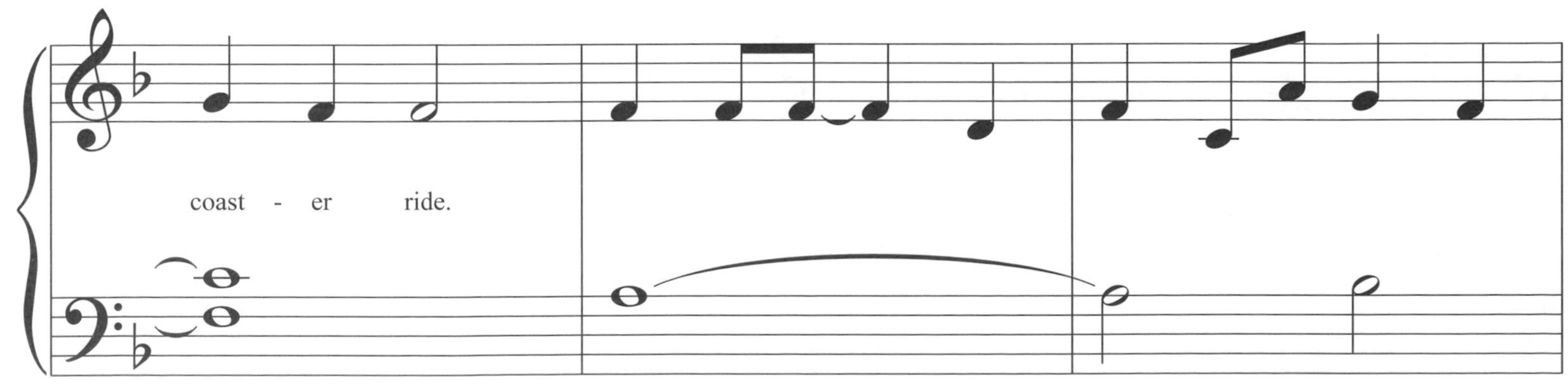
coast - er ride.

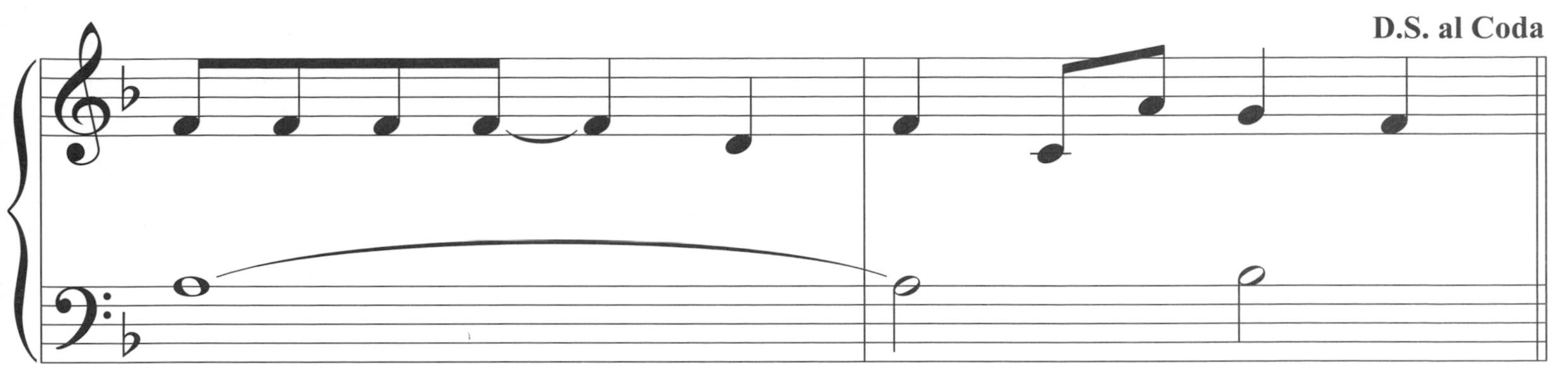
D.S. al Coda

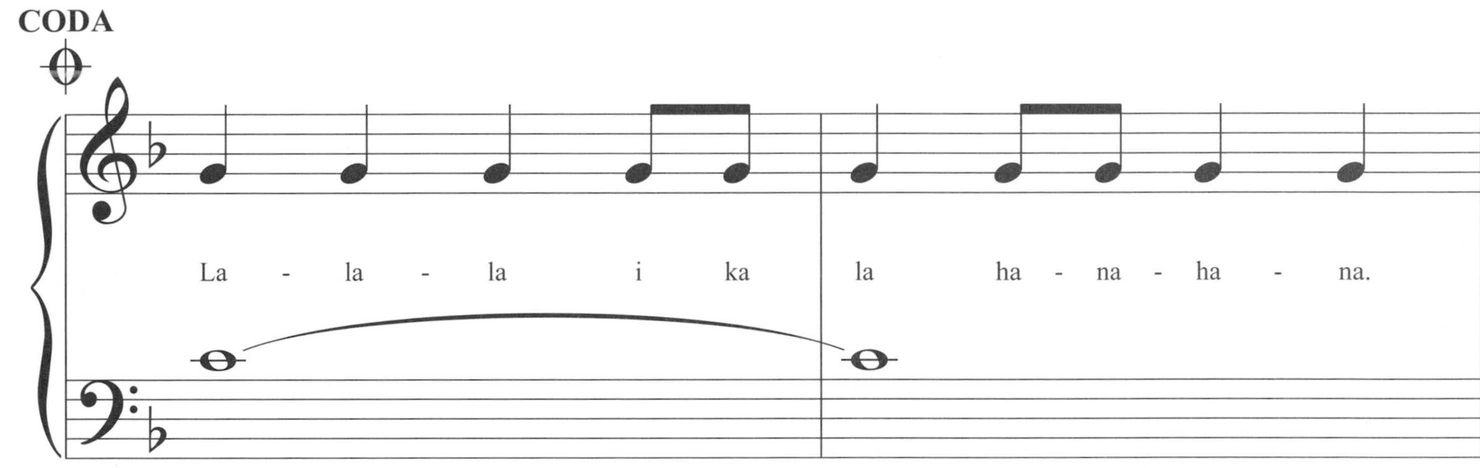
CODA
La - la - la i ka la ha - na - ha - na.

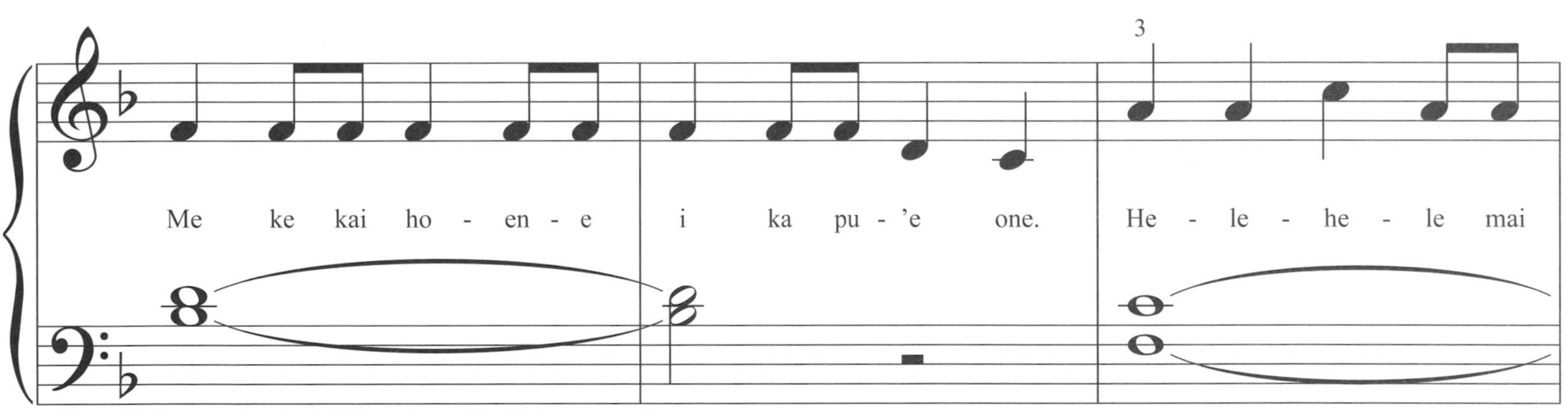
3
Me ke kai ho - en - e i ka pu - 'e one. He - le - he - le mai

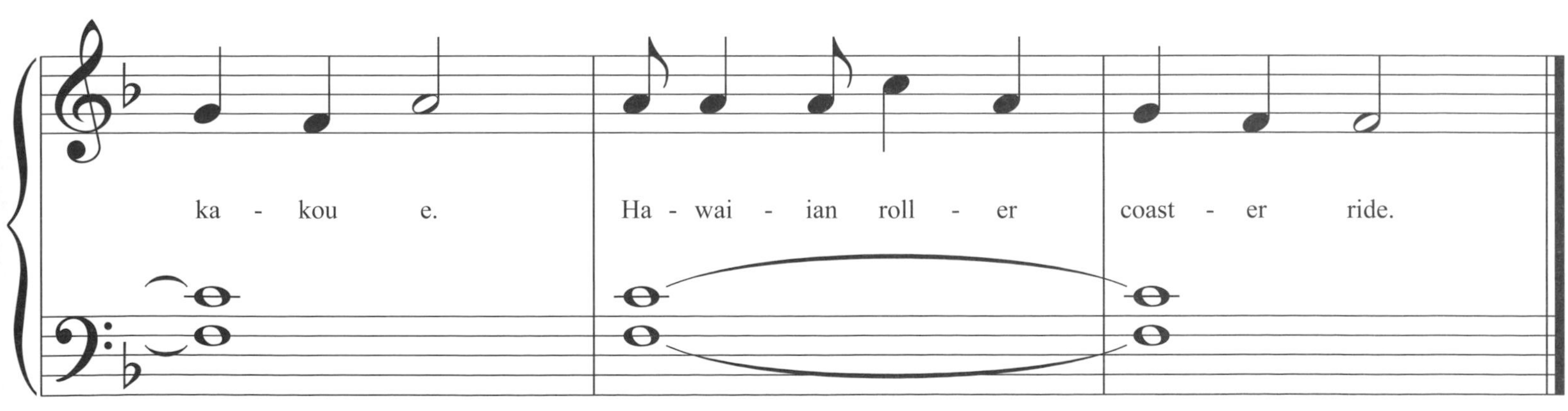
ka - kou e. Ha - wai - ian roll - er coast - er ride.

I JUST CAN'T WAIT TO BE KING

from THE LION KING

Music by ELTON JOHN
Lyrics by TIM RICE

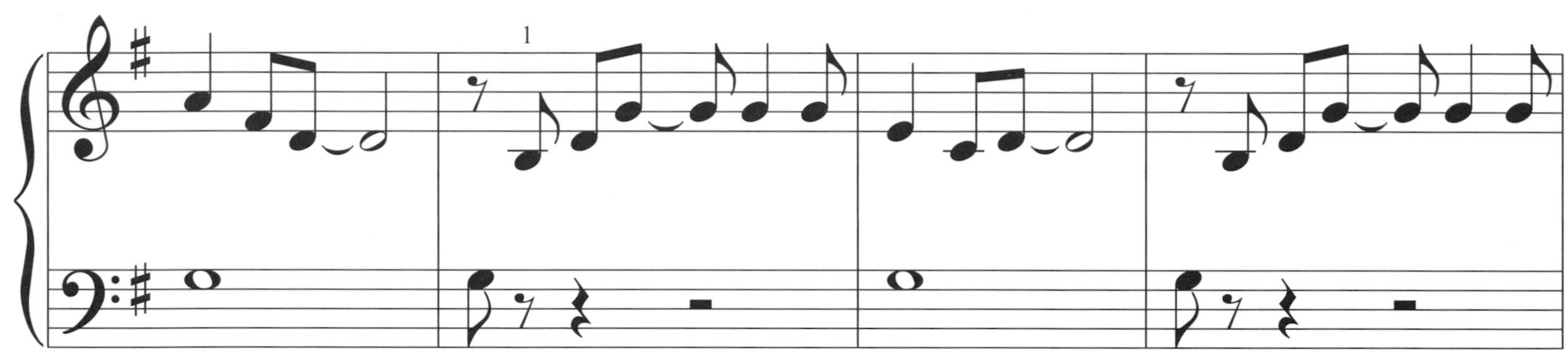

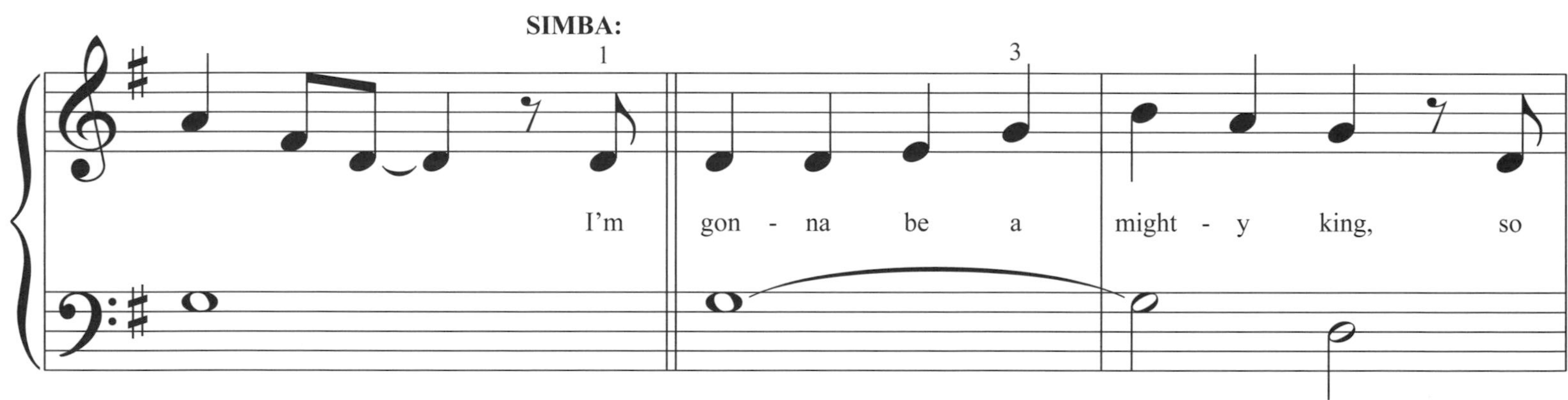

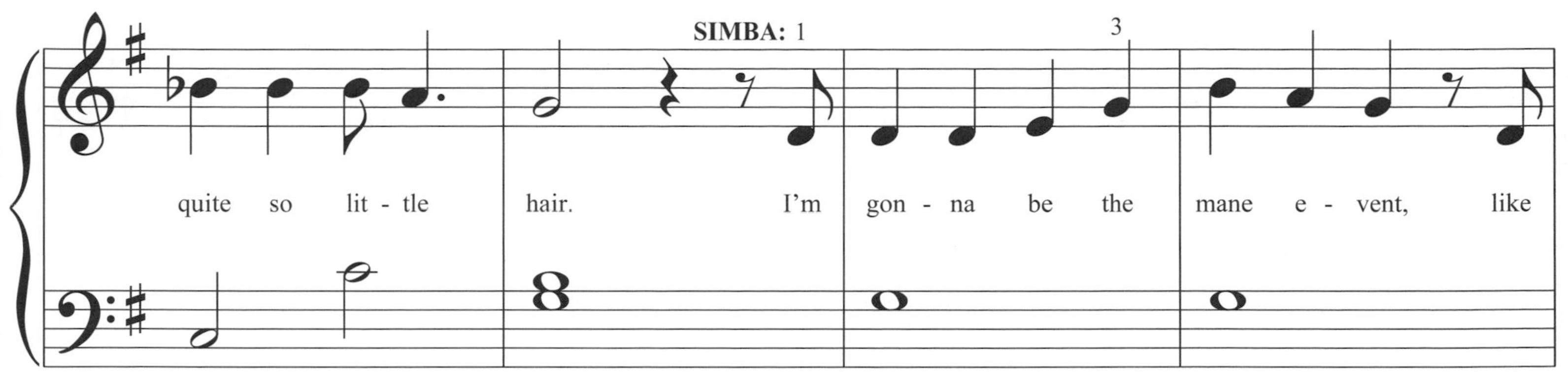
SIMBA: 1
3
quite so lit - tle
hair.
I'm
gon - na be the
mane e - vent, like

no king was be -
fore.
I'm
brush - ing up on
look - ing down. I'm

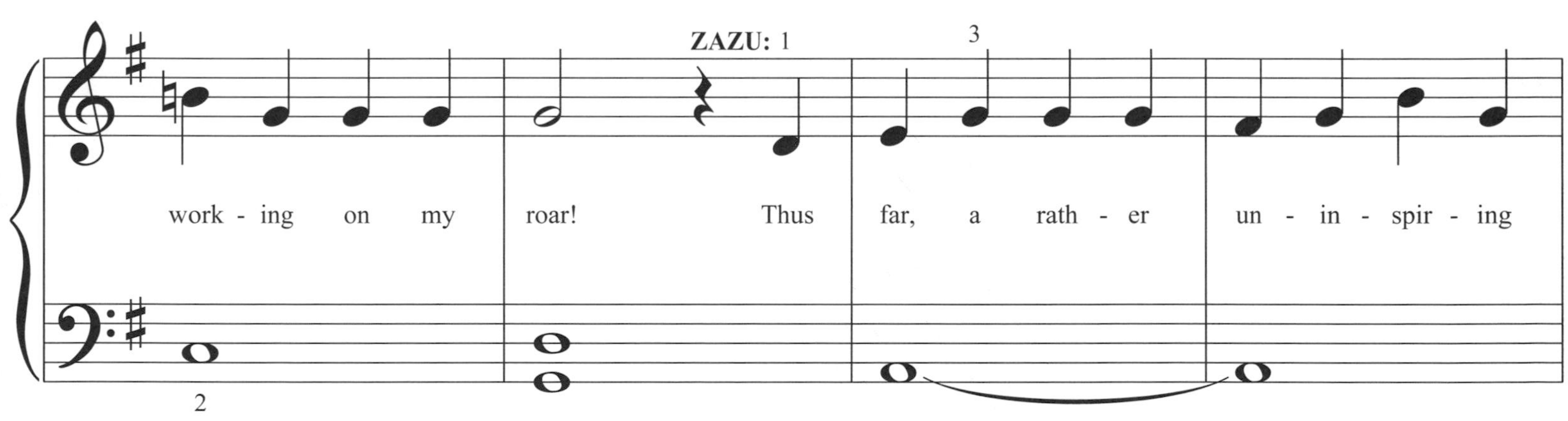
ZAZU: 1
3
work - ing on my
roar!
Thus
far, a rath - er
un - in - spir - ing
2

SIMBA:
thing.
Oh, I
just can't
wait to be

5
king!
ZAZU: (Spoken) You've
rather a long way to go,
young master! If you think...

SIMBA: 1
No one say - ing
"do this,"
ZAZU: (Spoken) Now,
when I said that,
no one say - ing

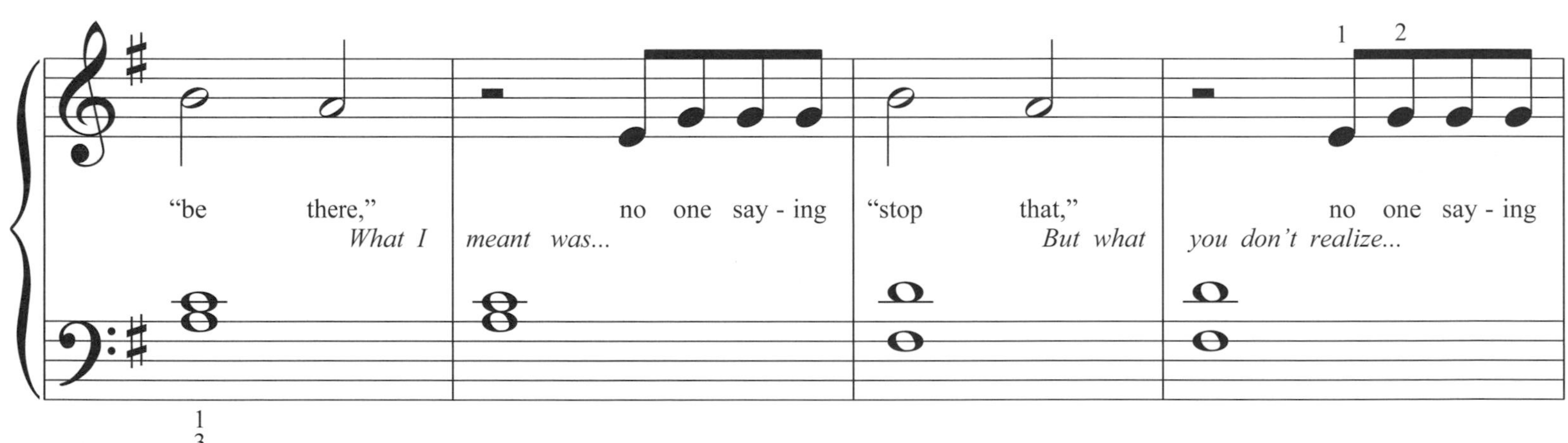
1 2
"be there,"
What I
meant was...
no one say - ing
"stop that,"
But what
you don't realize...
no one say - ing
1
3

"see here."
Now see here!
Free to run a - round all

day,
Well, that's
definitely out.
free to do it all my

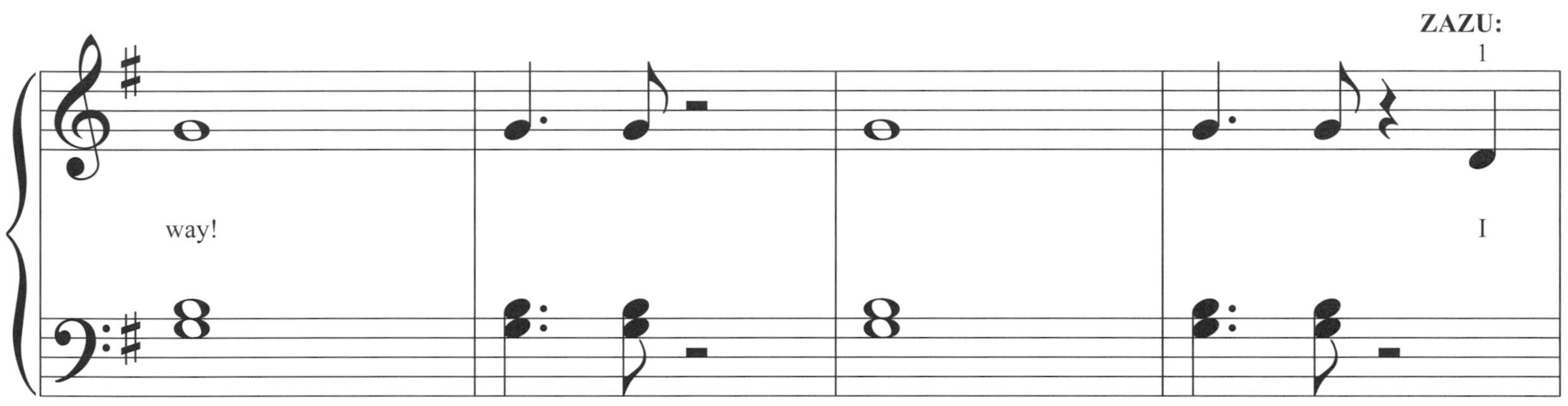
ZAZU:
way!
I

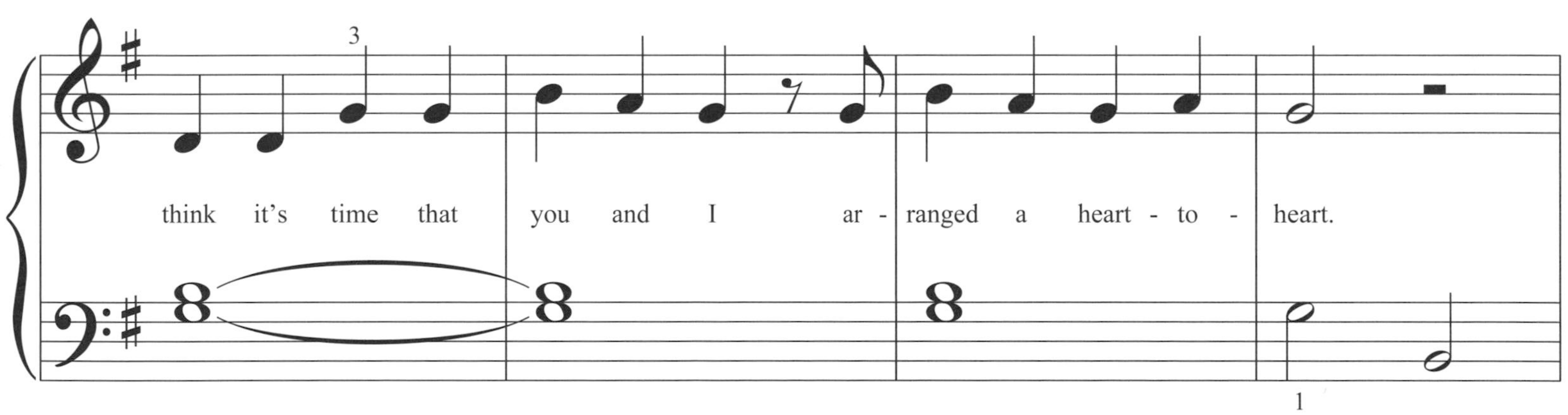
think it's time that you and I ar - ranged a heart - to - heart.

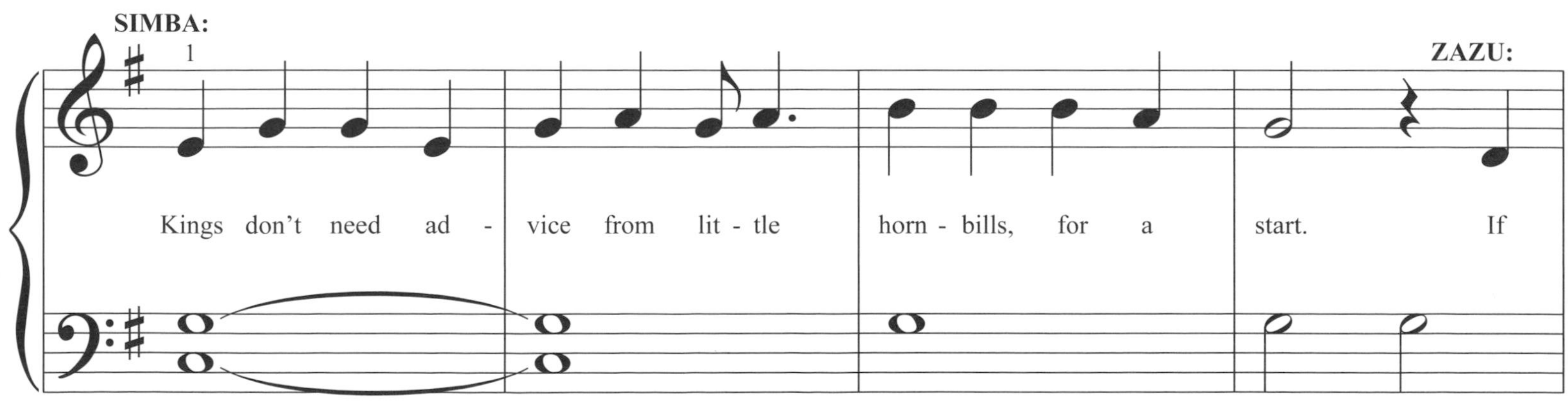
SIMBA:
Kings don't need ad - vice from lit - tle horn - bills, for a start.
ZAZU:
If

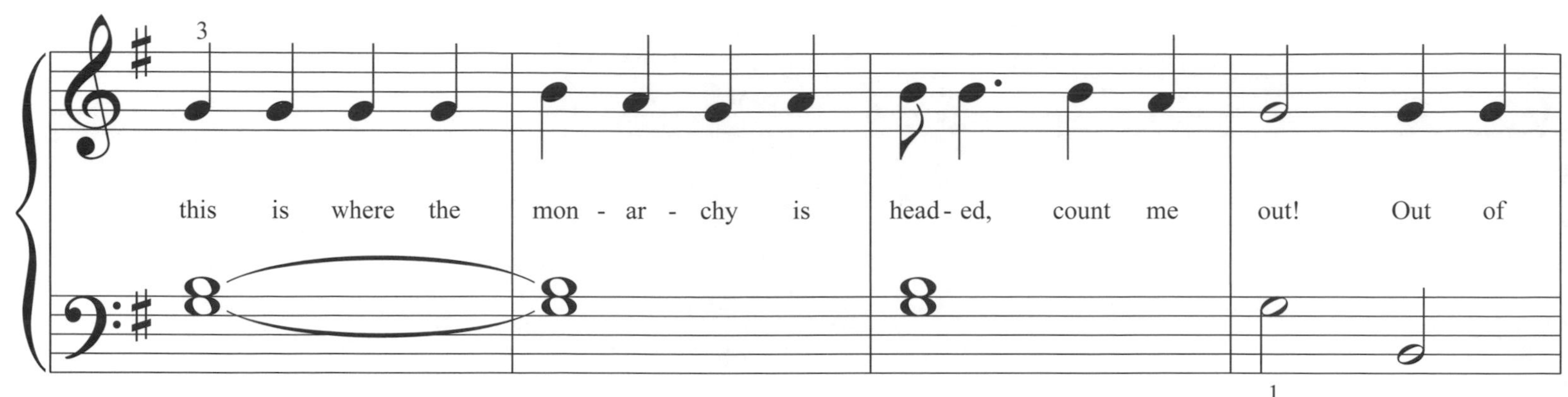
3
this is where the mon - ar - chy is head - ed, count me out! Out of
1

2
ser - vice, out of Af - ri - ca. I would - n't hang a - bout. This
4

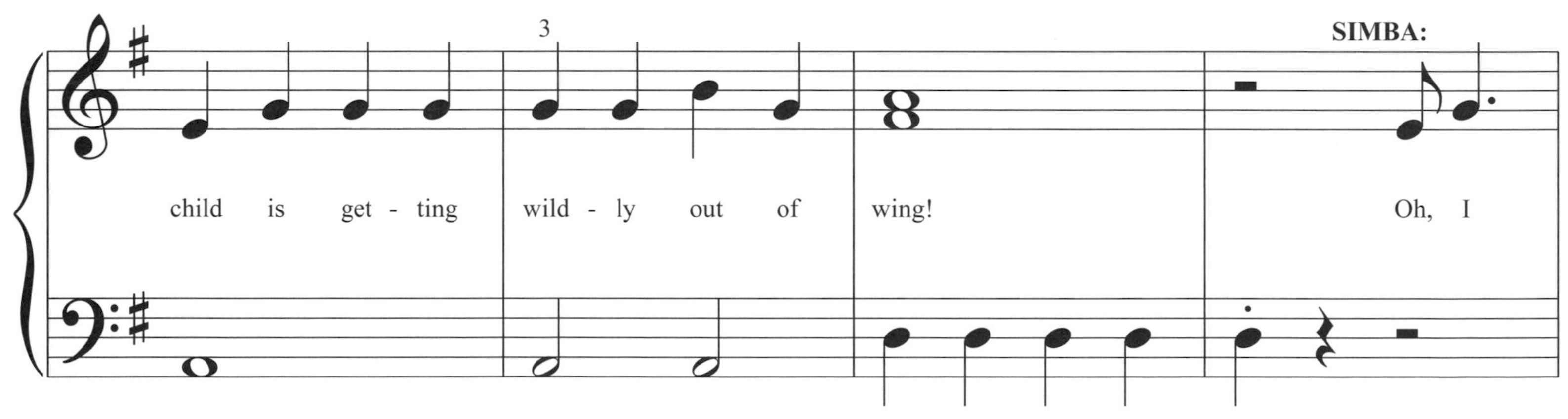
3
SIMBA:
child is get - ting wild - ly out of wing! Oh, I

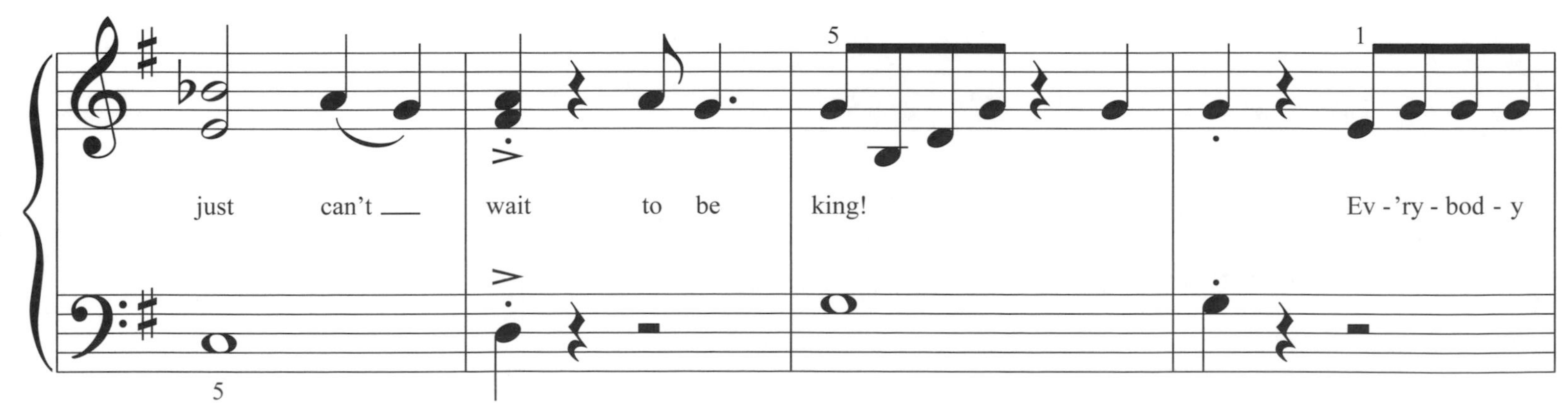
5
1
just can't wait to be king! Ev - 'ry - bod - y
5

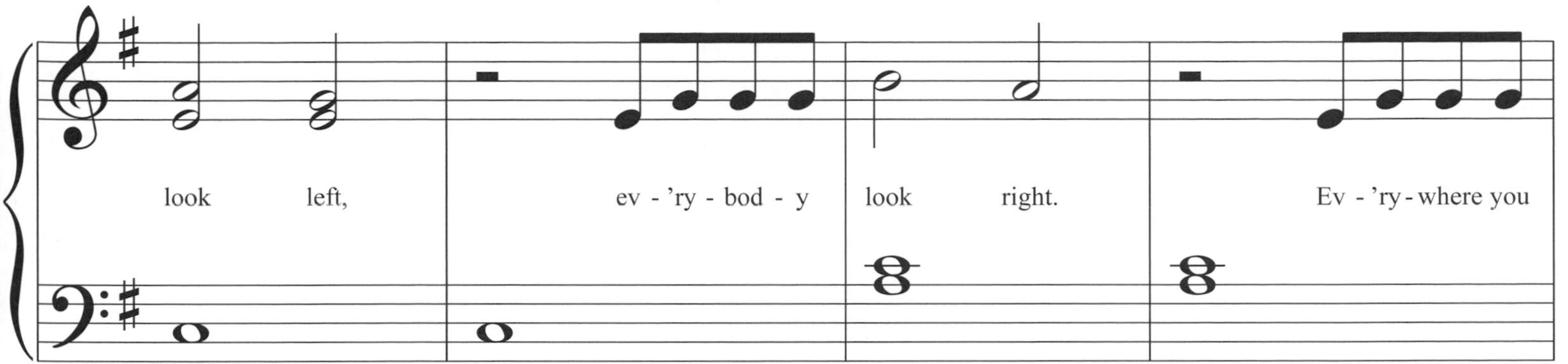
look left,
ev - 'ry - bod - y
look right.
Ev - 'ry - where you

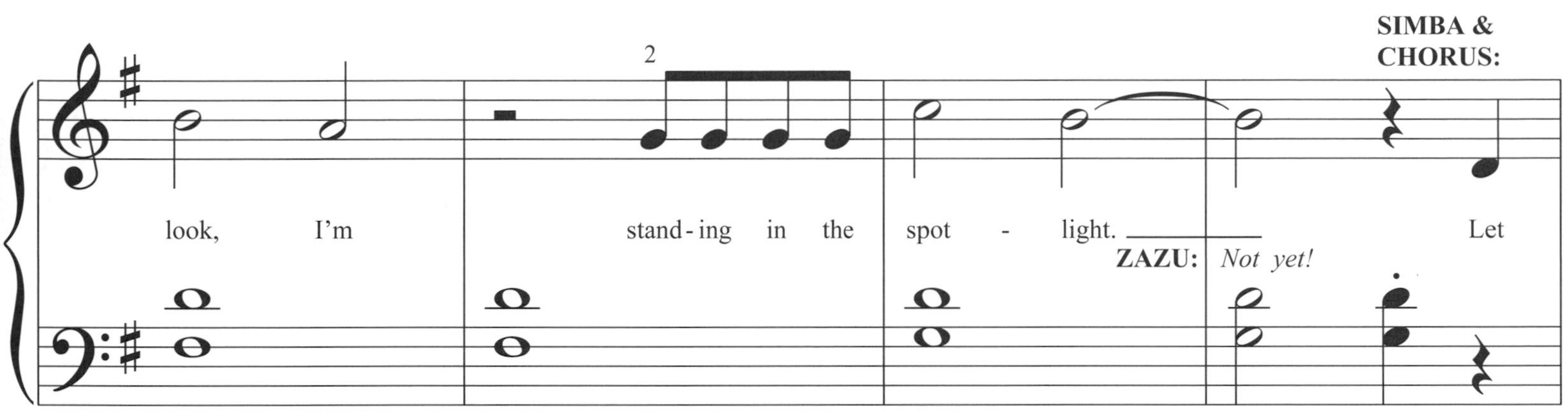
SIMBA & CHORUS:
2
look, I'm
stand - ing in the
spot - light.
Let
ZAZU: Not yet!

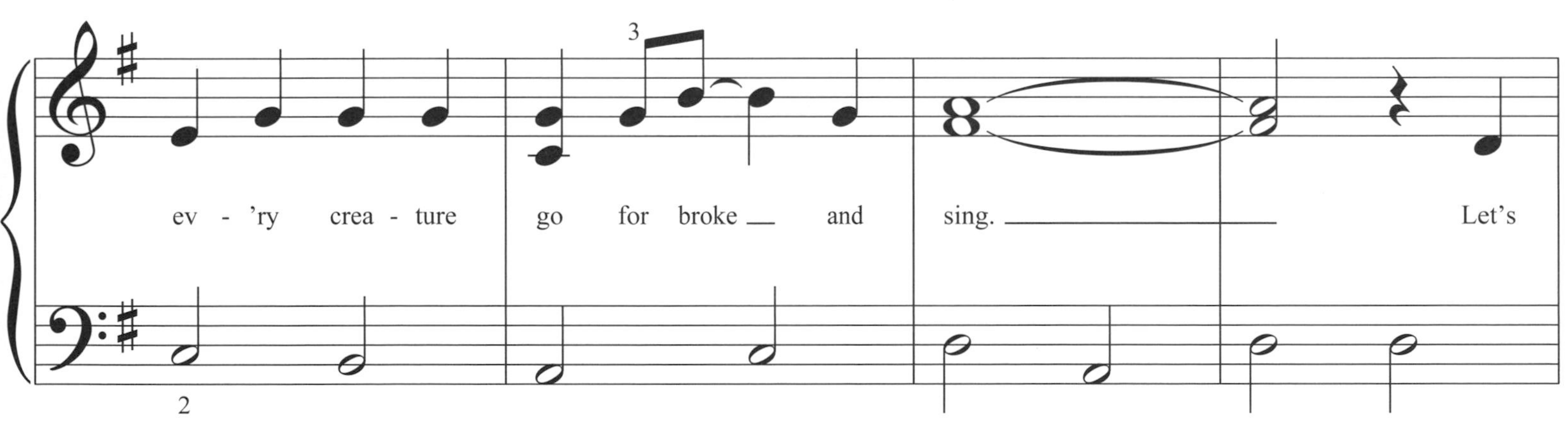
3
ev - 'ry crea - ture
go for broke and
sing.
Let's
2

hear it in the
herd and on the
wing.
It's

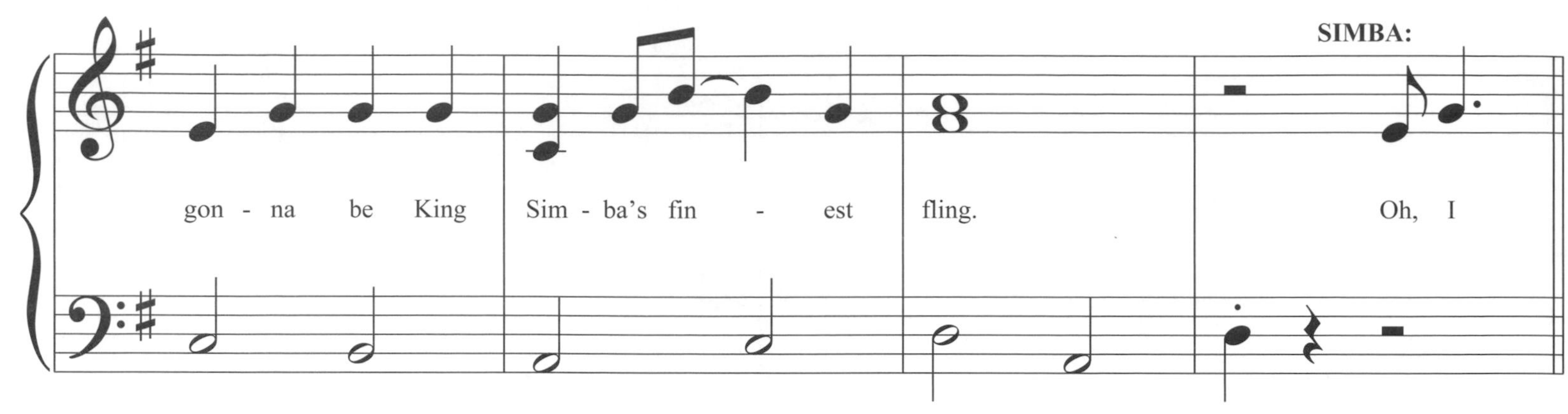
SIMBA:
gon - na be King Sim - ba's fin - est fling. Oh, I

just can't wait to be king! Oh, I

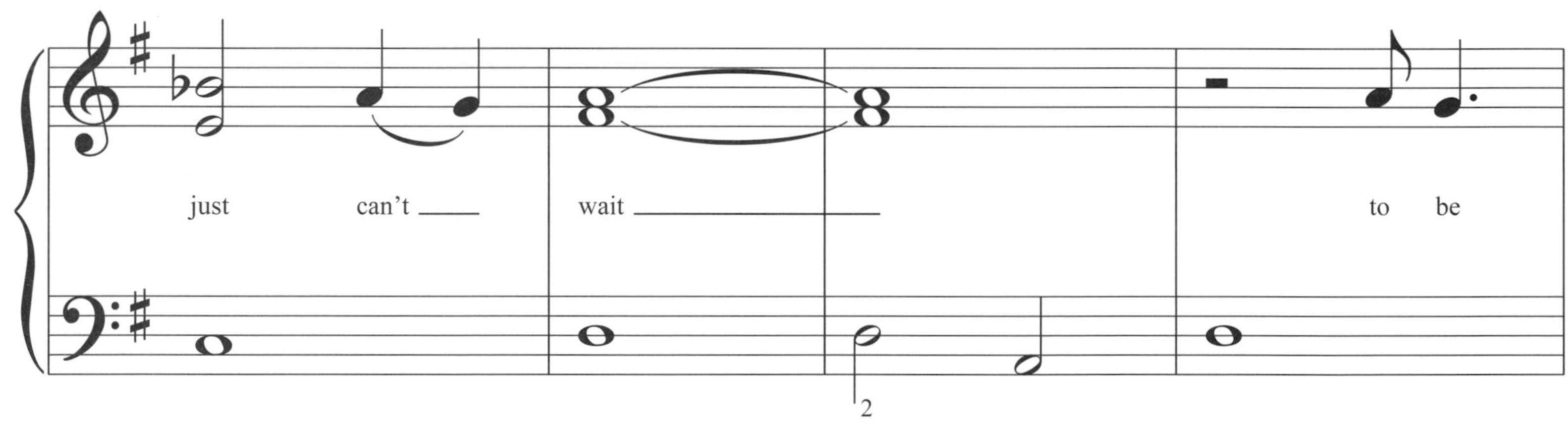
just can't wait to be
2

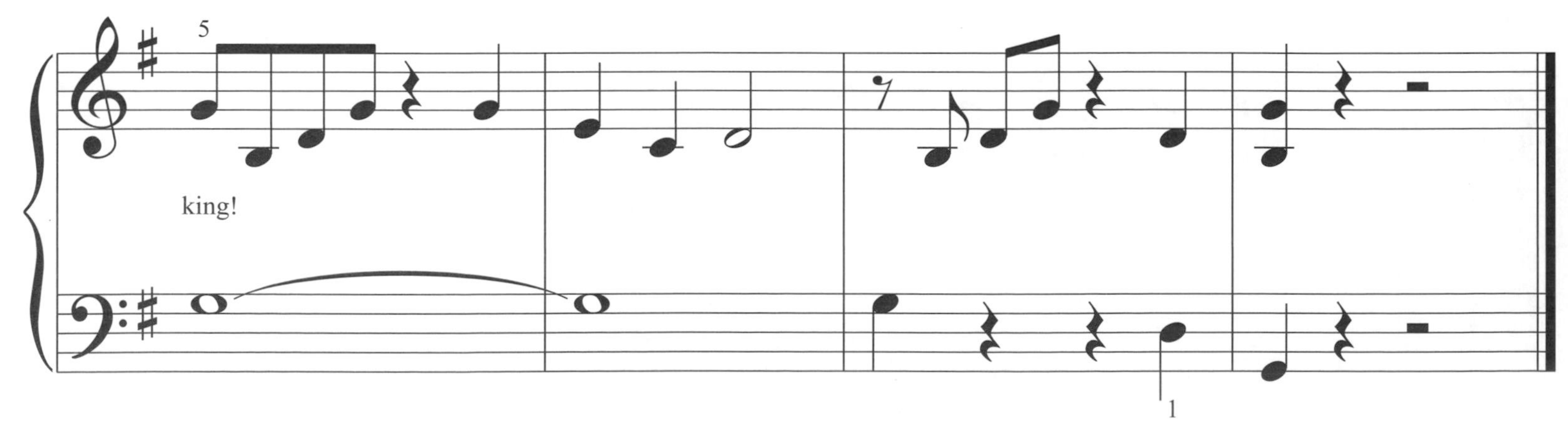
5
king!
1

IF I DIDN'T HAVE YOU

from MONSTERS, INC.

Music and Lyrics by
RANDY NEWMAN

3
4
Sulley: 'cause dreams do come true,
I would - n't have

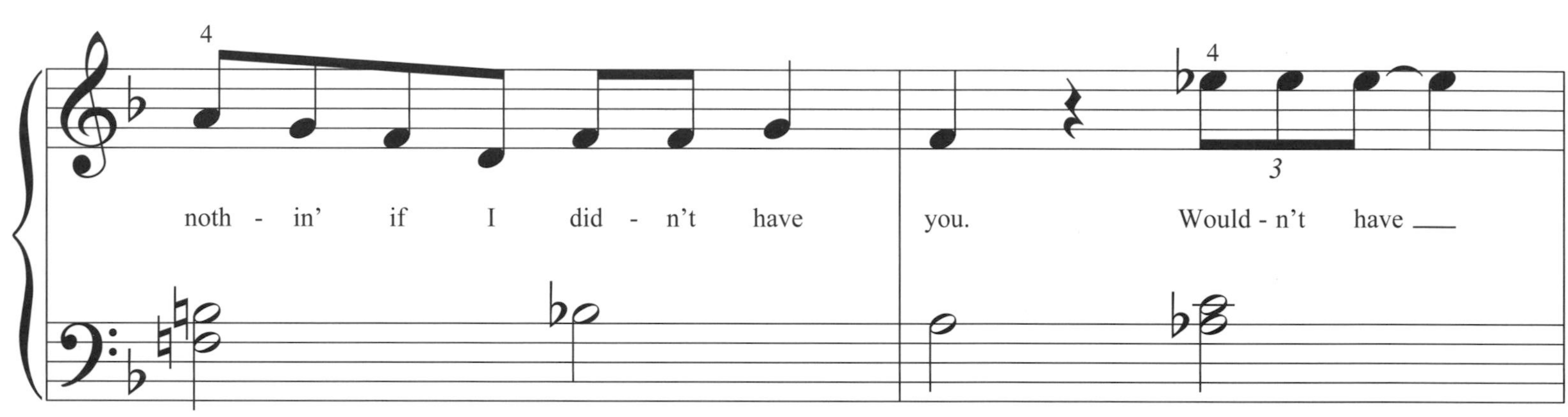
4
4
3
noth - in' if I did - n't have
you. Would - n't have

3
noth - in' if I did - n't have,
would - n't have

3
noth - in' if I did - n't have,
would - n't have

5
3
noth - in'.
Mike: For years I have
en - vied
(Instrumental) Mike: Yeah,
I wouldn't be nothin'
Sulley: Yes, I would-n't be
noth - in'

your grace and your
charm.
Ev - 'ry - one
Sulley: Aw, man. Mike: if I didn't
have you to serve.
I'm just a punky little
if I did - n't have
you.
I would-n't know where to
1

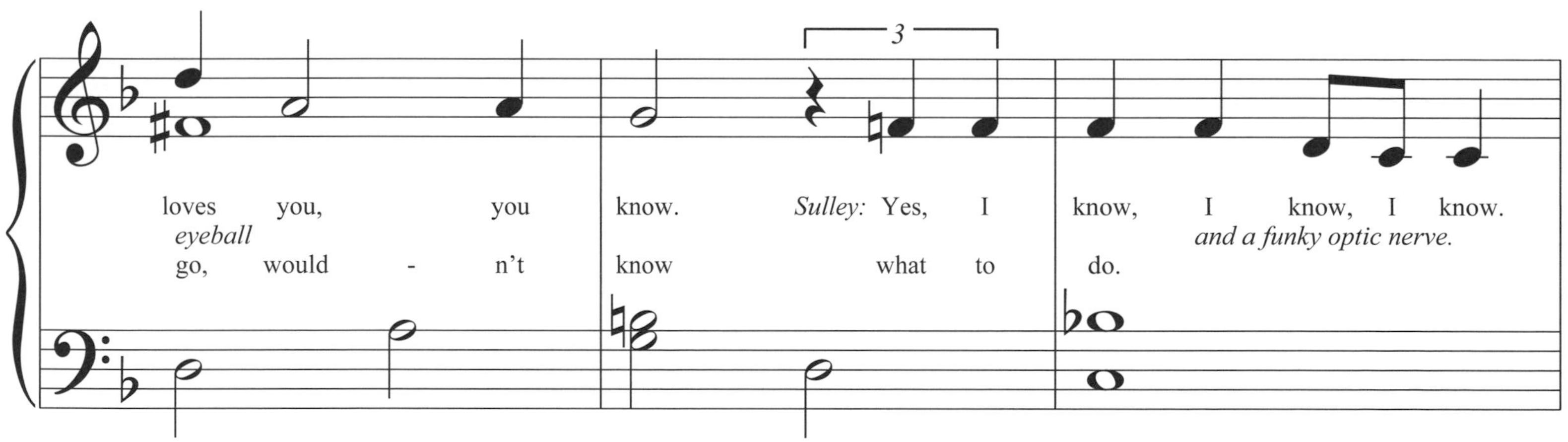
3
loves you, you
know.
Sulley: Yes, I
know, I know, I know.
eyeball
and a funky optic nerve.
go, would - n't
know what to
do.

1
3
1
3
Mike: But I must ad -
mit it,
big guy, you al - ways come
Hey, I n-never
told you this,
some-times I get a lit - tle
Both: I don't have to
say it,
we both know it's

through. I would - n't have
blue, Sulley: Looks good on you. Mike: but I would - n't have
true. I would - n't have

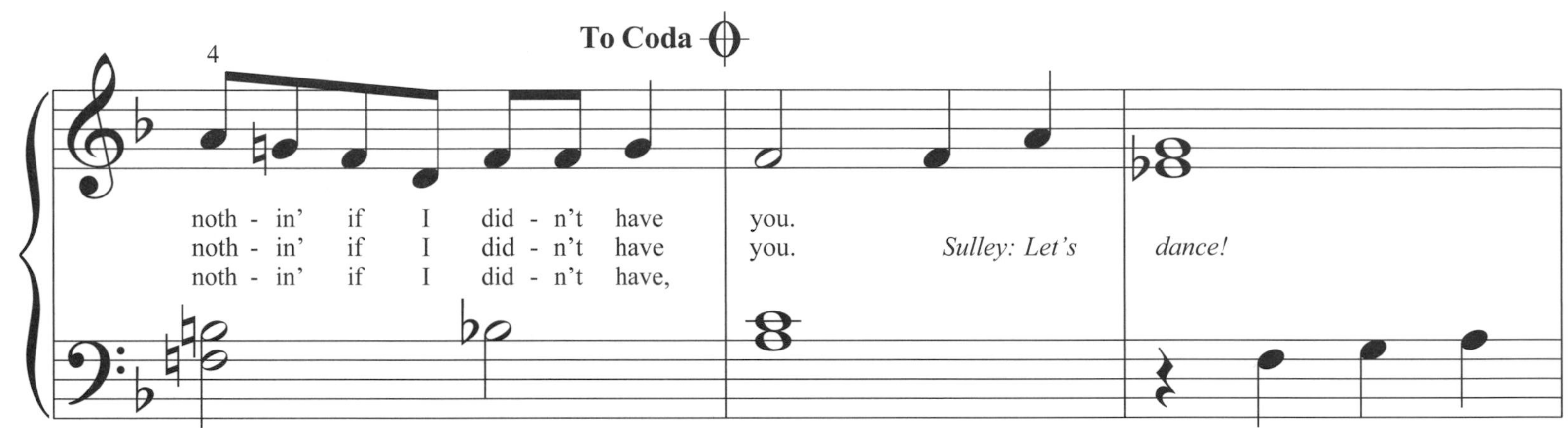
To Coda
4
noth - in' if I did - n't have you.
noth - in' if I did - n't have you. Sulley: Let's dance!
noth - in' if I did - n't have,

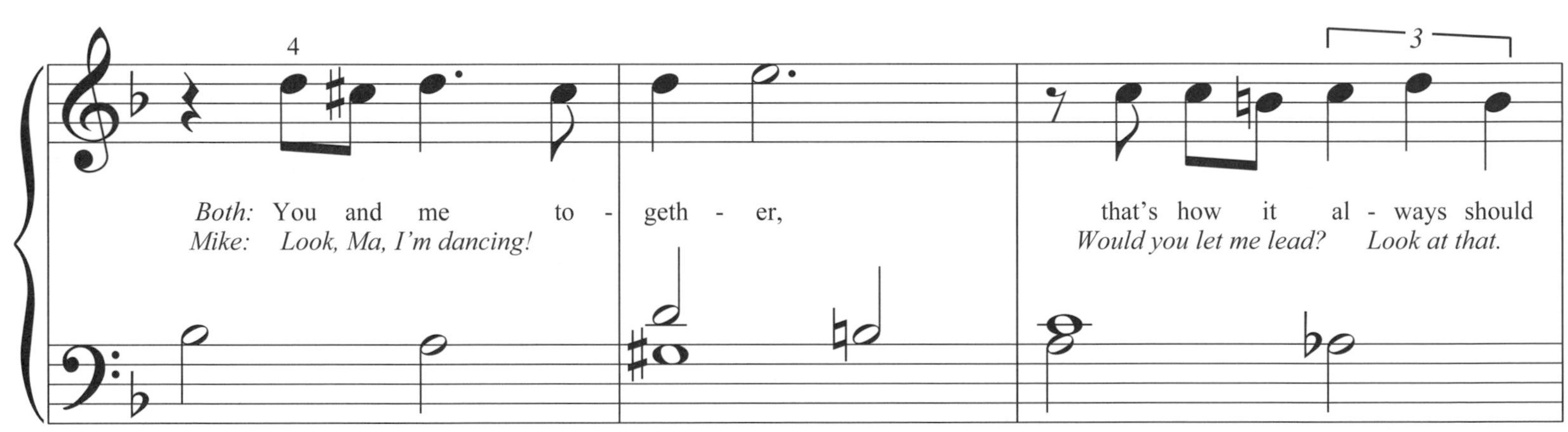
4
3
Both: You and me to - geth - er, that's how it al - ways should
Mike: Look, Ma, I'm dancing! Would you let me lead? Look at that.

4
1
3
3
be. One with - out the oth - er don't mean
It's true! Big guys are light on their feet. Don't you dare dip me. Don't you dare dip me.

1.
noth - ing to me,
noth - ing to me.
2.
D.S. al Coda
Don't you dare dip me.
Ow! I should've stretched.
CODA
I would - n't have
noth - in' if I did - n't have,
I would - n't have
noth - in' if I did - n't have

3
you.
Would - n't
have
noth - in'
if
I
did - n't
have

4
2
3
you.
Mike: One more
time.
It worked!
Sulley: Don't
have
to

3
say
it
'cause
we
both
know
it's
true.
3

4
Both: I
would - n't
have
noth - in'
if
I
did - n't
have,

4
I would - n't have
noth - in' if I did - n't have,

4
I would - n't have
noth - in' if I did - n't have

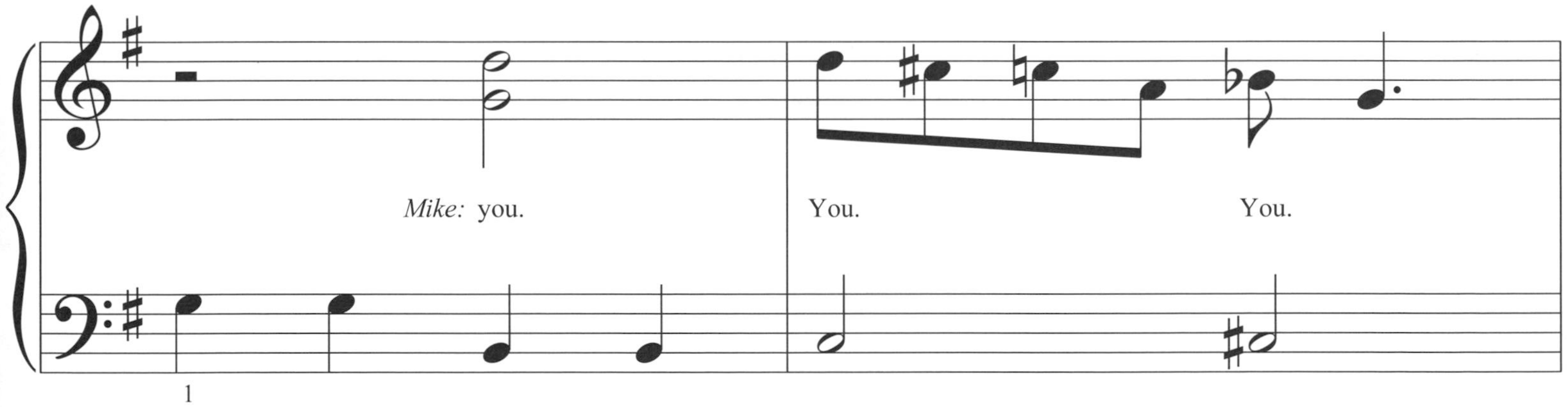
Mike: you.
You.
You.
1

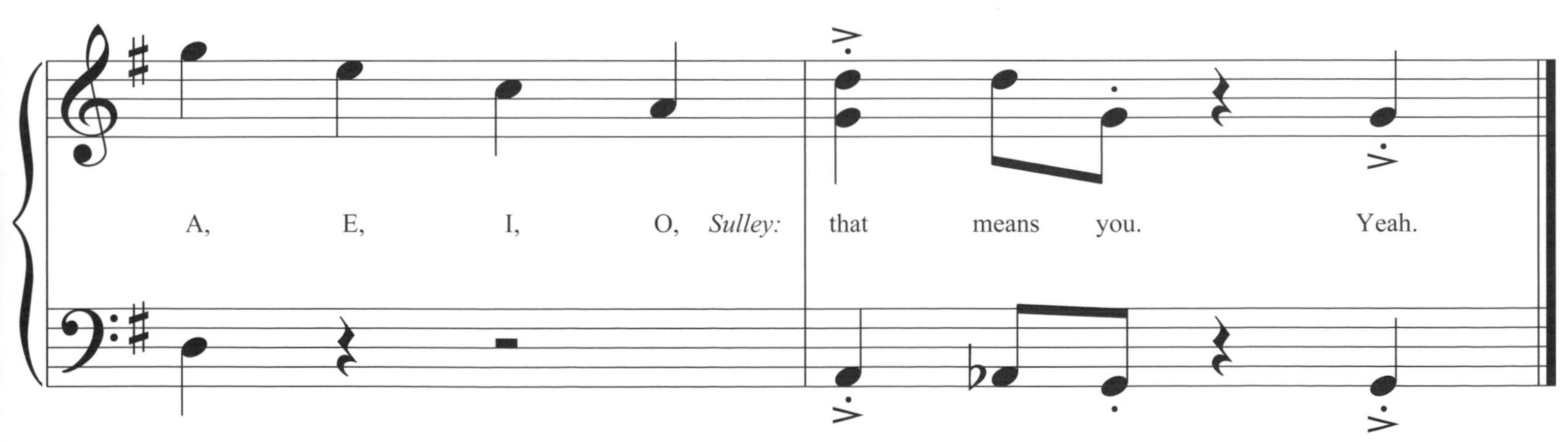
A, E, I, O, Sulley: that means you. Yeah.

I SEE THE LIGHT

from TANGLED

Music by ALAN MENKEN
Lyrics by GLENN SLATER

Moderately

2.
3
Stand - ing here, it's oh, so clear I'm where I'm meant to

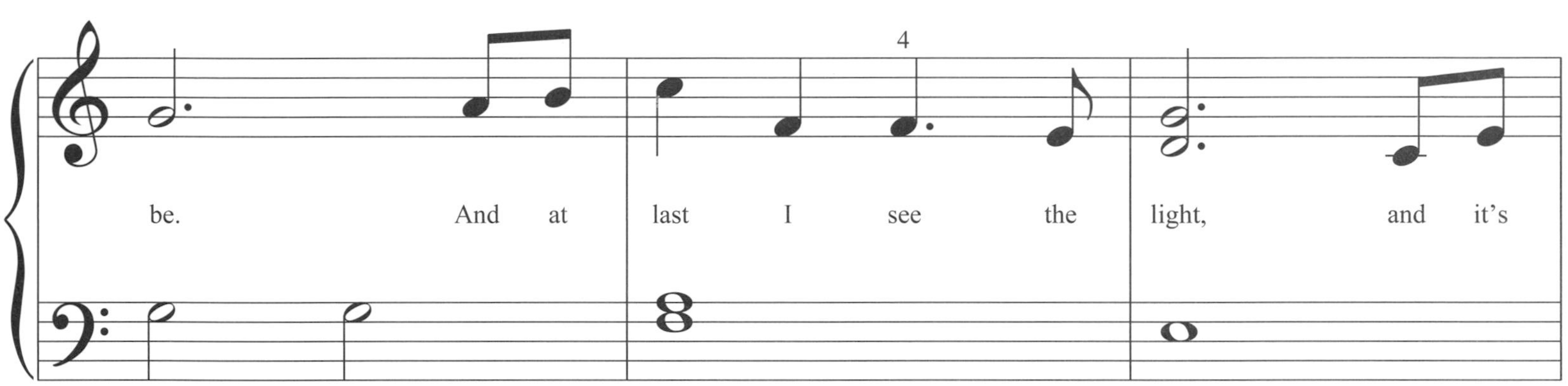
4
be. And at last I see the light, and it's

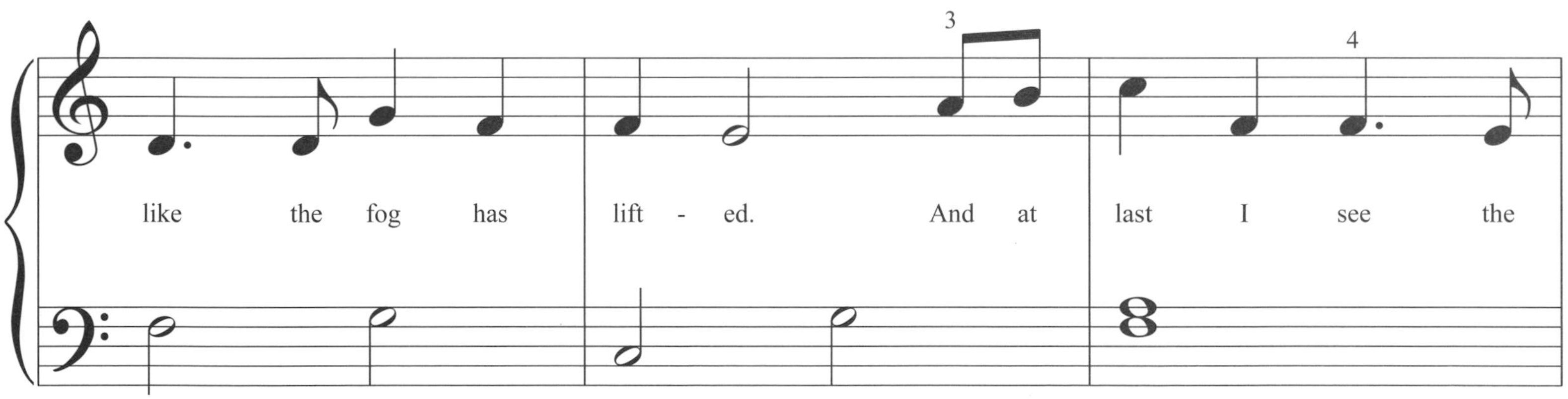
3
4
like the fog has lift - ed. And at last I see the

3
light, and it's like the sky is new. And it's

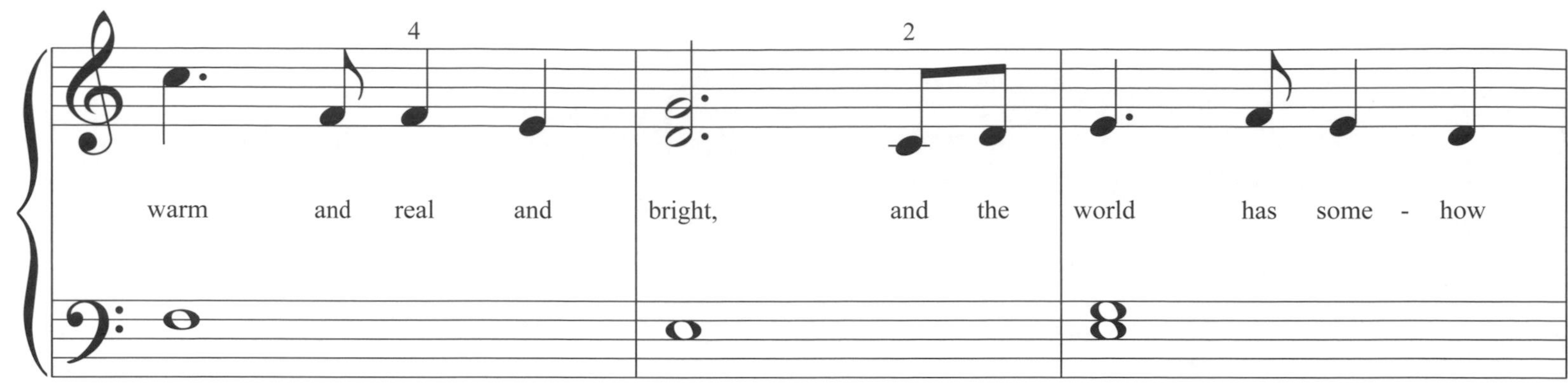
4
2
warm and real and bright, and the world has some - how

shift - ed. All at once,
5

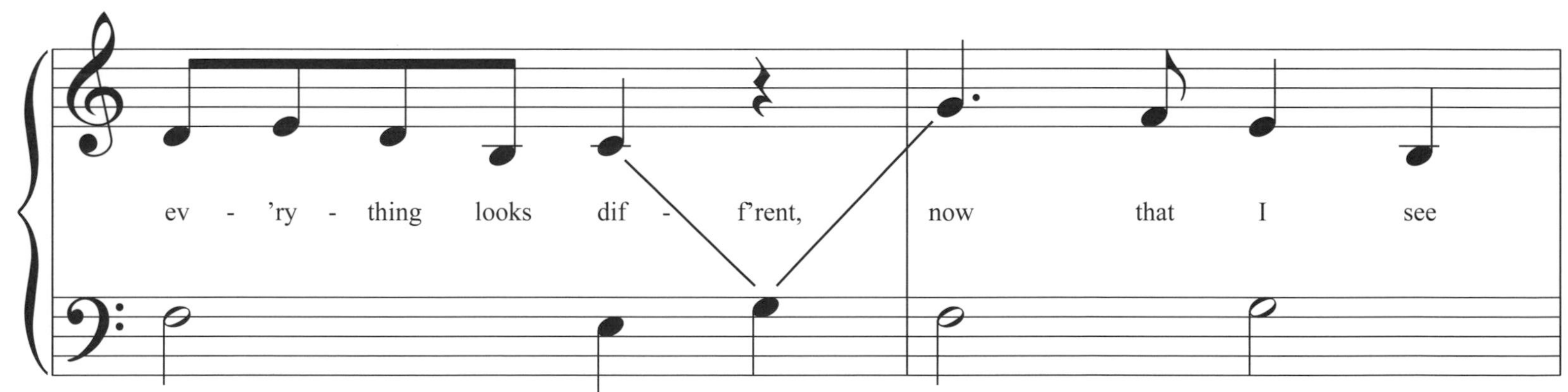
ev - 'ry - thing looks dif - f'rent, now that I see

5
you. All those days,
1

chas - ing down a day - dream. All those years liv - ing in a blur.

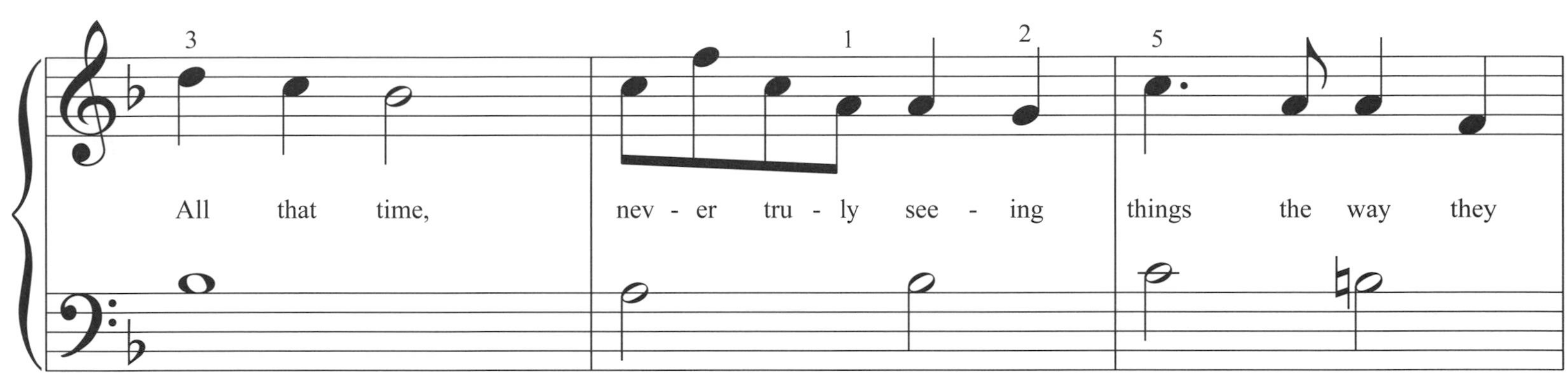
3
1
2
5
All that time, nev - er tru - ly see - ing things the way they

4
were. Now she's here, shin - ing in the star - light.
2

5
3
Now she's here; sud - den - ly I know: if she's here, it's

crys - tal clear I'm where I'm meant to go. And at
2
4

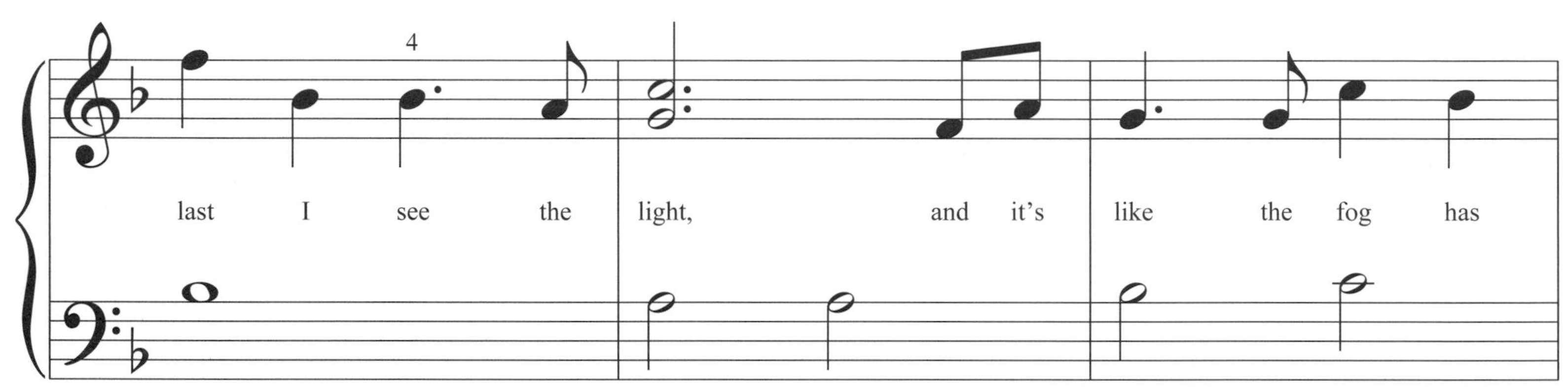
4
last I see the light, and it's like the fog has

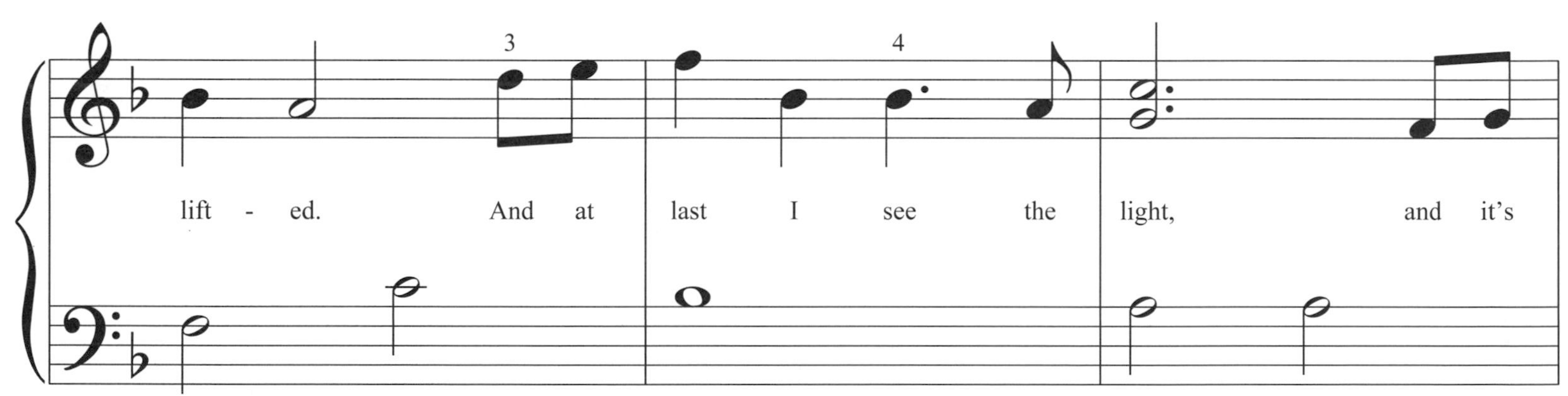
3
4
lift - ed. And at last I see the light, and it's

1
4
1
2
like the sky is new. And it's warm and real and

1 2 4
bright, and the world has some - how shift - ed.

1 4 4
All at once, ev - 'ry - thing is dif - f'rent,

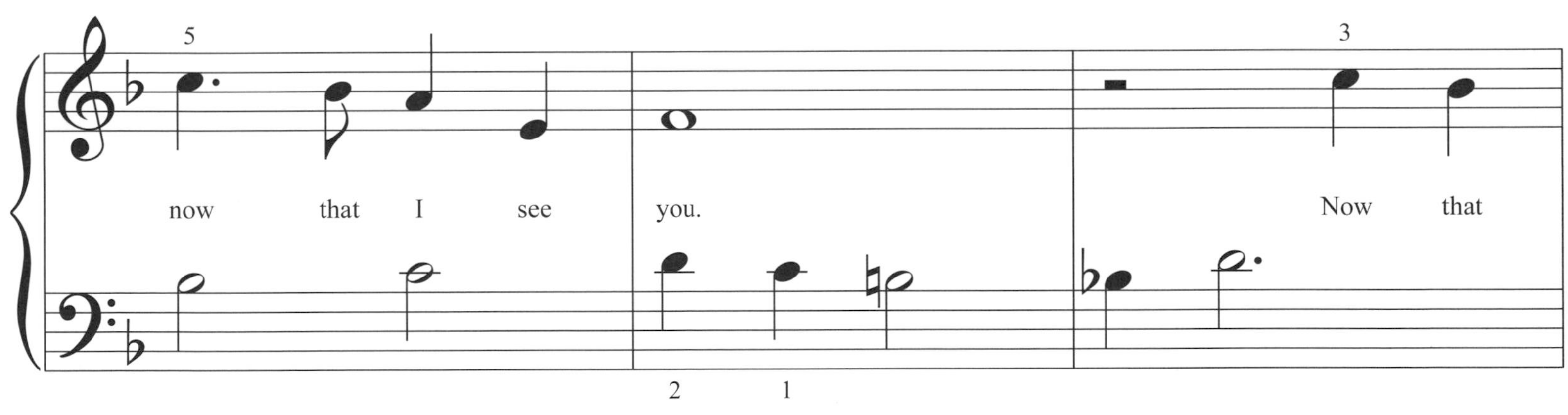
5 3
now that I see you. Now that
2 1

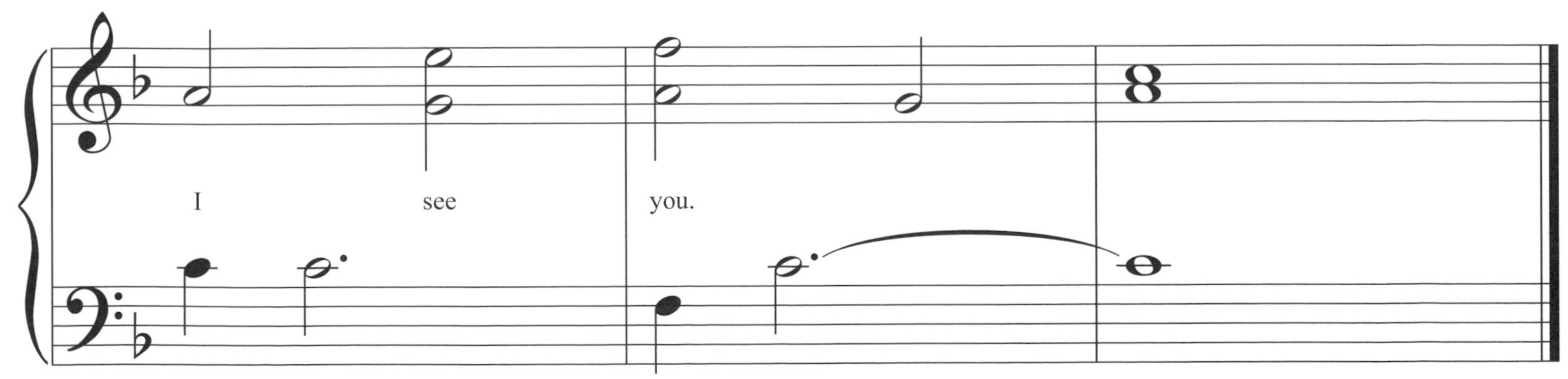
I see you.

INTO THE OPEN AIR

from BRAVE

Words and Music by
ALEXANDER L. MANDEL

Moderate Folk Waltz

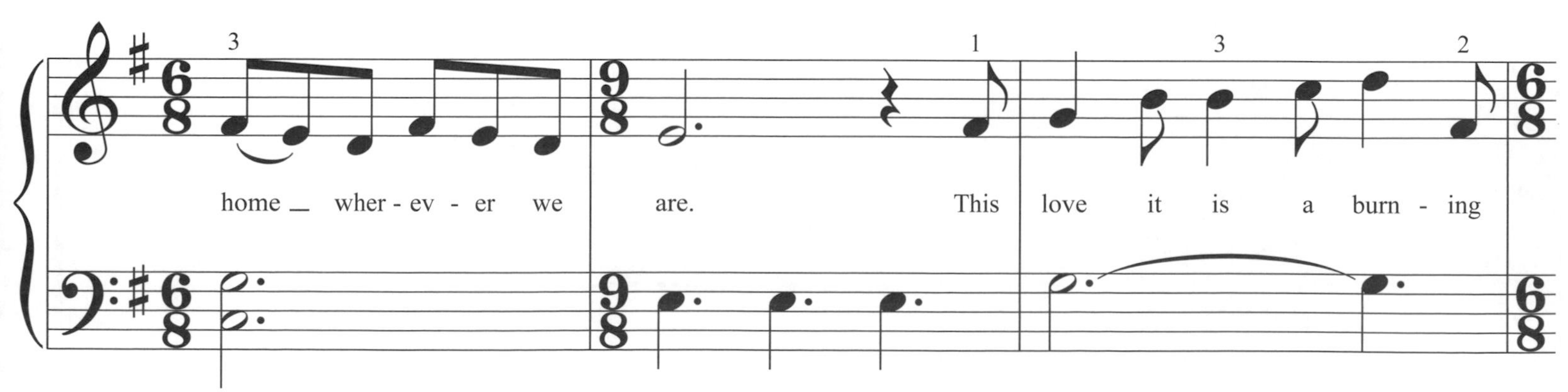

2
1
sun.
Shine your light on the things that we've done.
done. I

2
tried to speak to you
ev - 'ry day but each

1
4
word we spoke the
wind blew a - way.

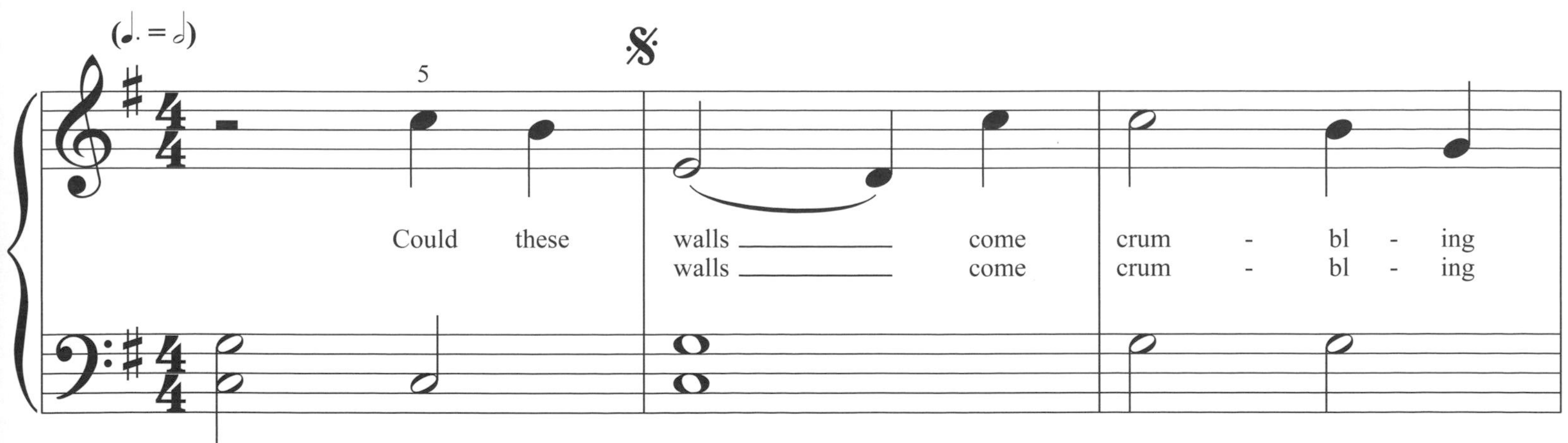
5
Could these
walls come crum - bl - ing
walls come crum - bl - ing

4
down?
down.
I want to
And I can
feel ___ my
feel ___ my

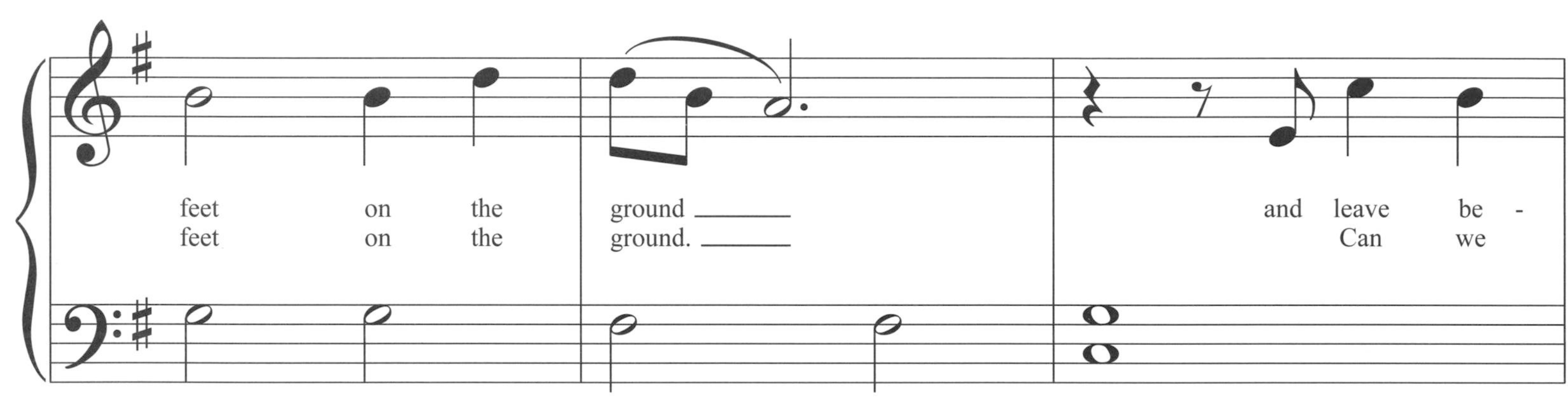
feet on the
feet on the
ground ___
ground. ___
and leave be -
Can we

To Coda
4
hind ___ this
car - ry this
pris - on we
love that we
share.
Step in -

to the
o - pen air. ___

How did we let it come to this?
What we've just tast - ed we some-how still miss.
How will it feel when this day is

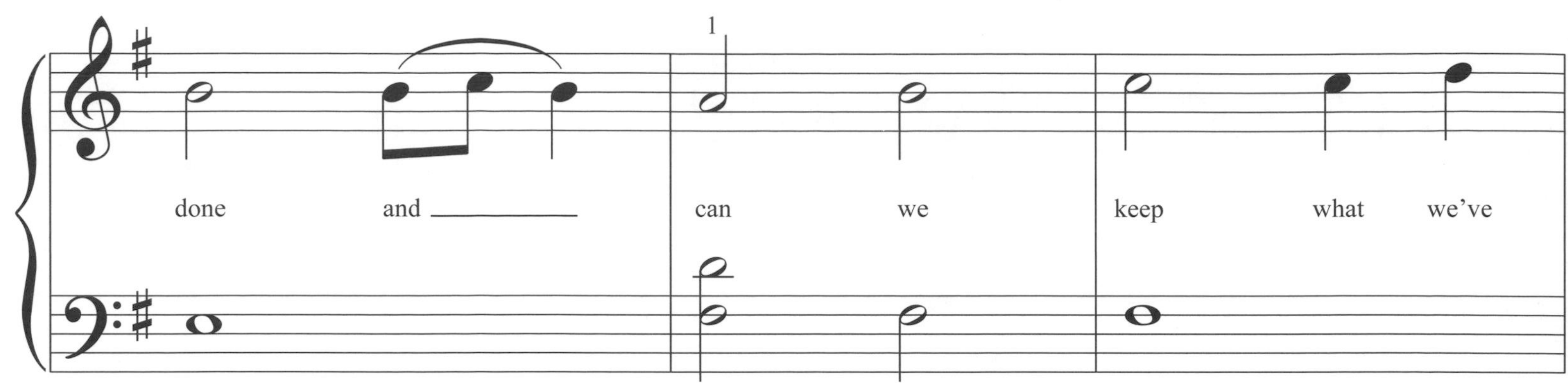
1
done and
can we
keep what we've

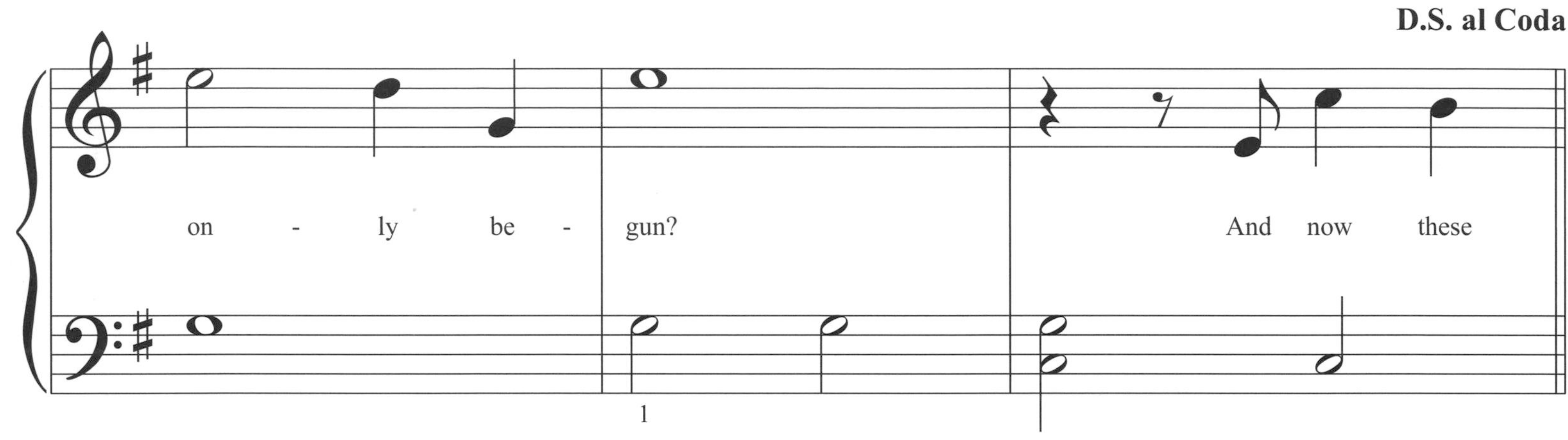
D.S. al Coda
on - ly be - gun?
And now these
1

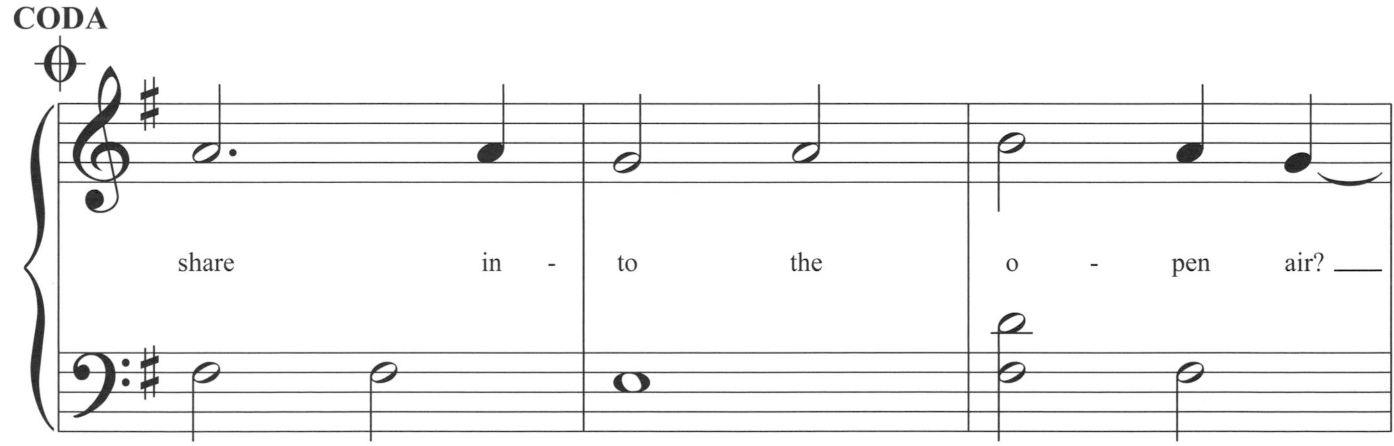
CODA
share in - to the o - pen air?

In - to the

o - pen air. In -
(𝅗𝅥 = 𝅘𝅥.)
to the o - pen air.
This
love it is a burn - ing sun.

IT'S ALL RIGHT

featured in SOUL

Words and Music by
CURTIS MAYFIELD

Moderately

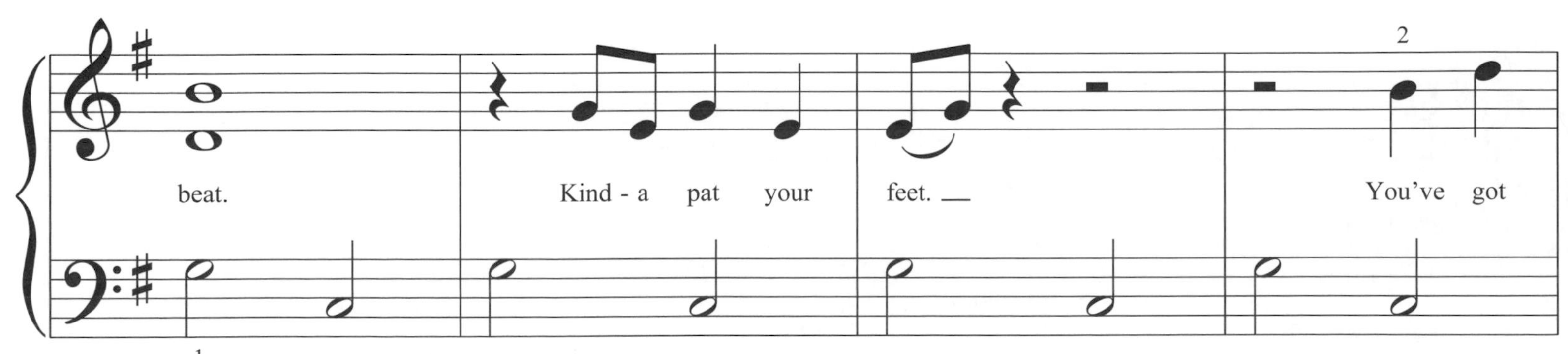

soul, and ev - 'ry - bod - y
knows that it's all
right, whoa, it's all
5

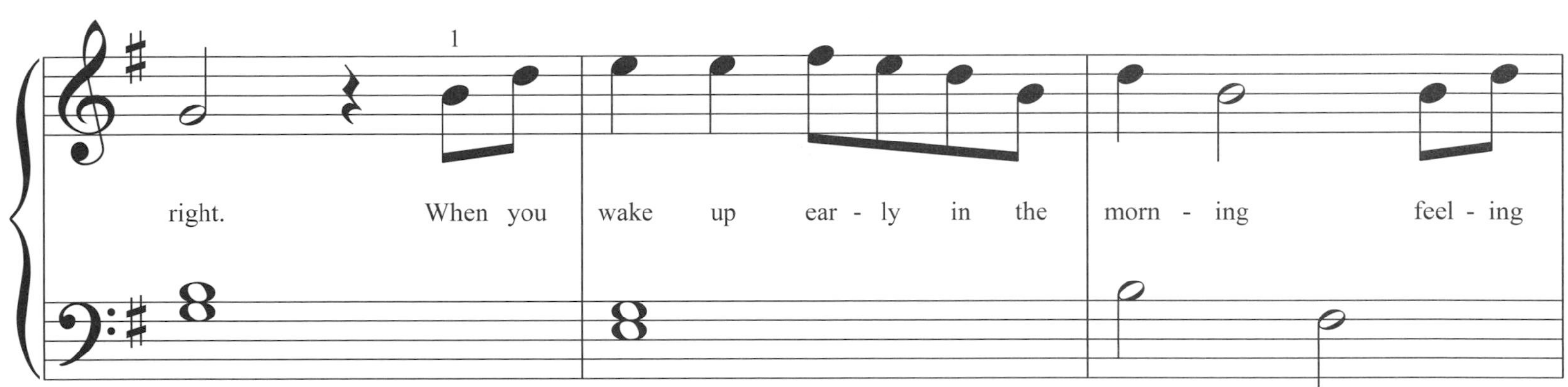
1
right. When you
wake up ear - ly in the
morn - ing feel - ing

sad like so man - y oth - ers
do, just
hum a lit - tle soul,

make life your goal, and
sure - ly some-thing's got - ta come to
you. Say it's all
3

right.
Say it's all
right.
It's all

5
right.
Have a good
time, 'cause it's all
right, whoa, it's all
5

right. Now ev - 'ry - bod - y clap your
hands.
Give your - self a
8

chance. _
You've got
soul.
Ev - 'ry - bod - y
5

knows that it's all right, whoa, it's all right. Now ev - 'ry - bod - y clap your

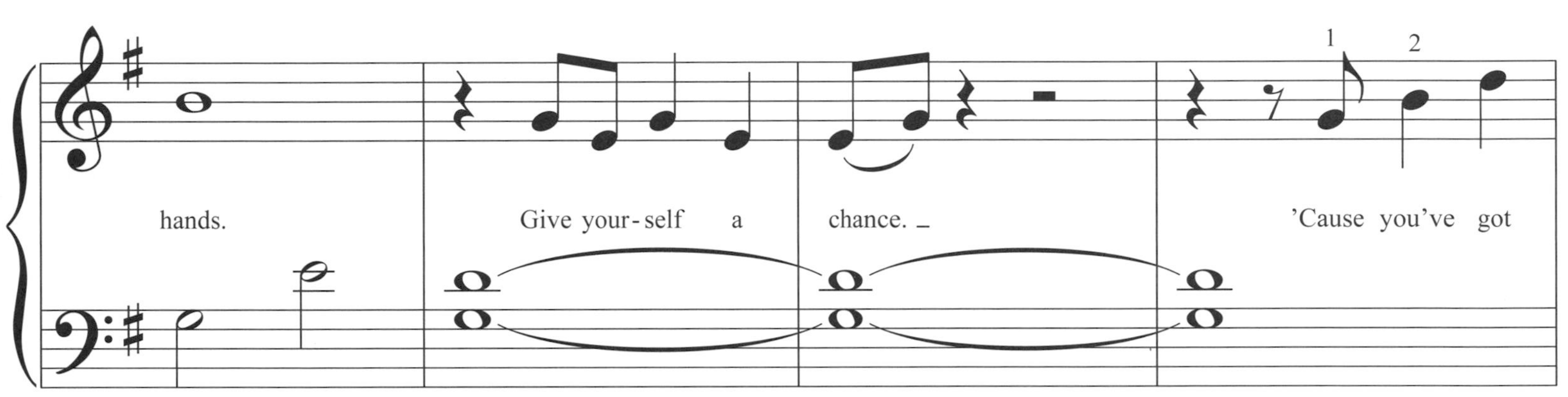
1 2
hands. Give your - self a chance. _ 'Cause you've got

3 2 3 2
soul. You've got soul. You've got

2
soul, and ev - 'ry - bod - y knows that it's all right.

LEAD THE WAY

from RAYA AND THE LAST DRAGON

Music and Lyrics by
JHENÉ AIKO

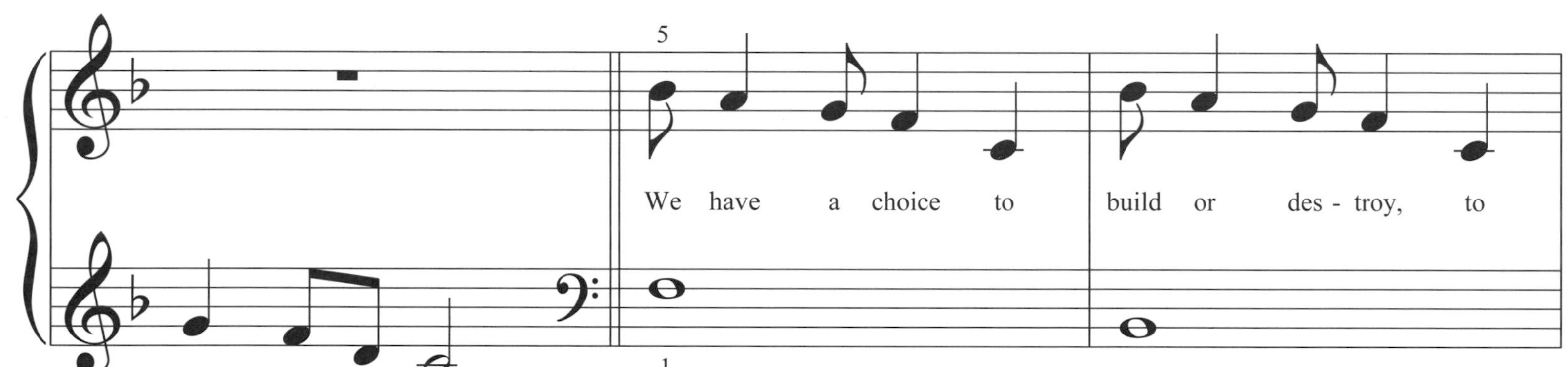

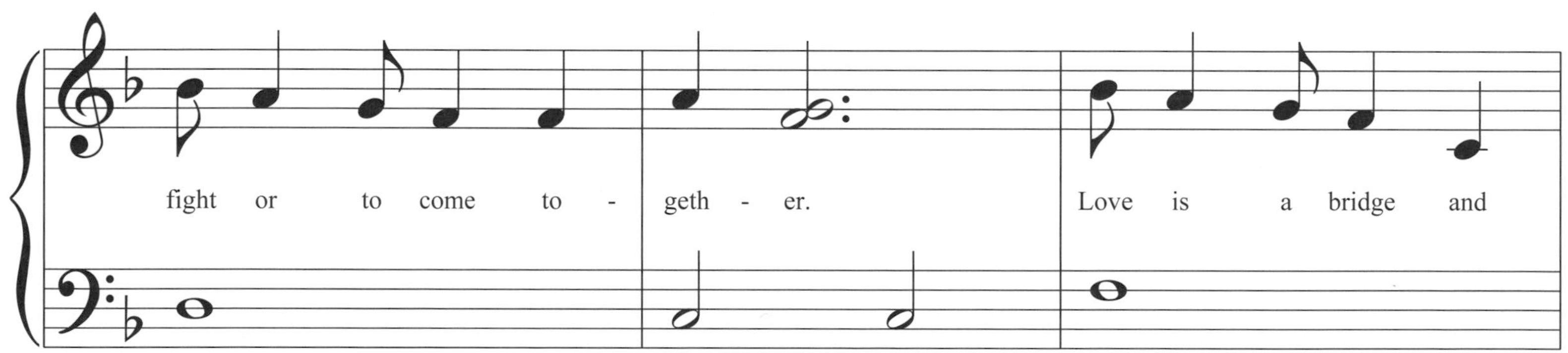

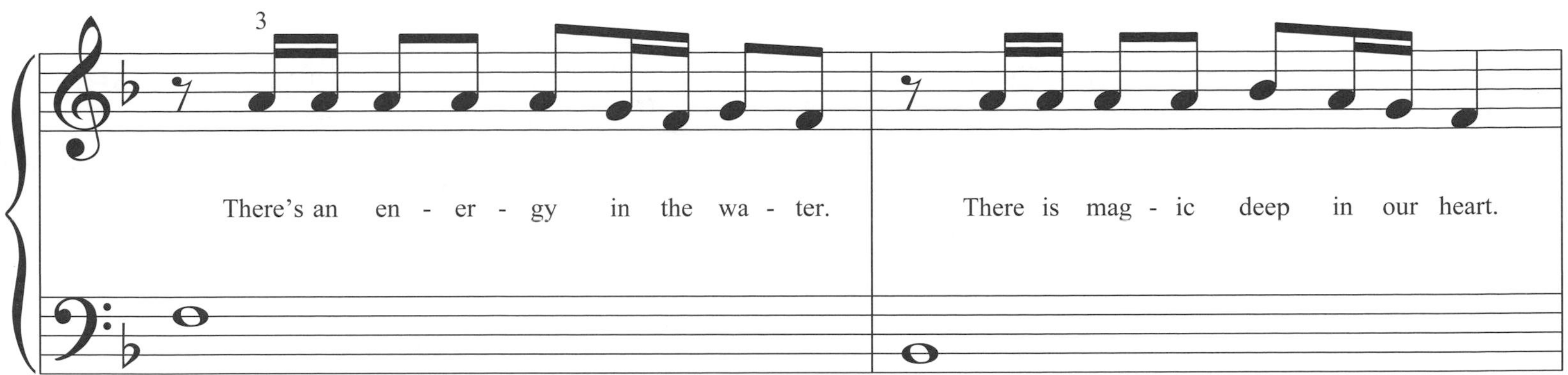
3
There's an en - er - gy in the wa - ter.
There is mag - ic deep in our heart.

There's a leg - a - cy that we hon - or
when we bring the light to the dark.

4
What - ev - er brings us to - geth - er
2
can nev - er tear us a - part.

We be - come strong - er than ev - er
1
when we just trust.

When we just trust.
When we just trust.

When we just trust.

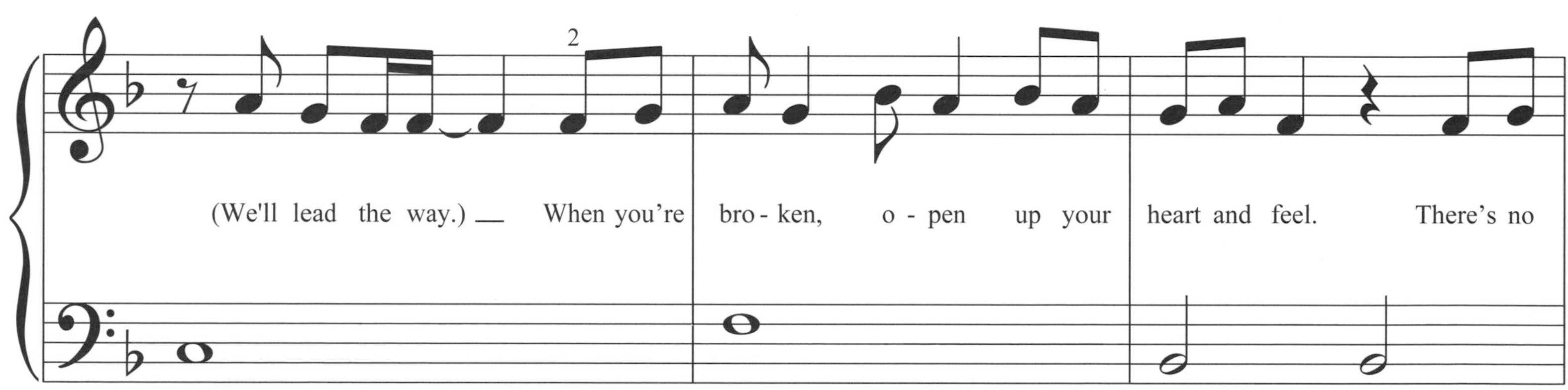
2
(We'll lead the way.) When you're bro - ken, o - pen up your heart and feel. There's no

dif- f'rence; we're all fam - 'ly here. De - spite all of our doubts, all our

4
ups and downs, there is nev - er real - ly an - y - thing to fear.

There's an en - er - gy in the wa - ter. There is mag - ic deep in our heart.

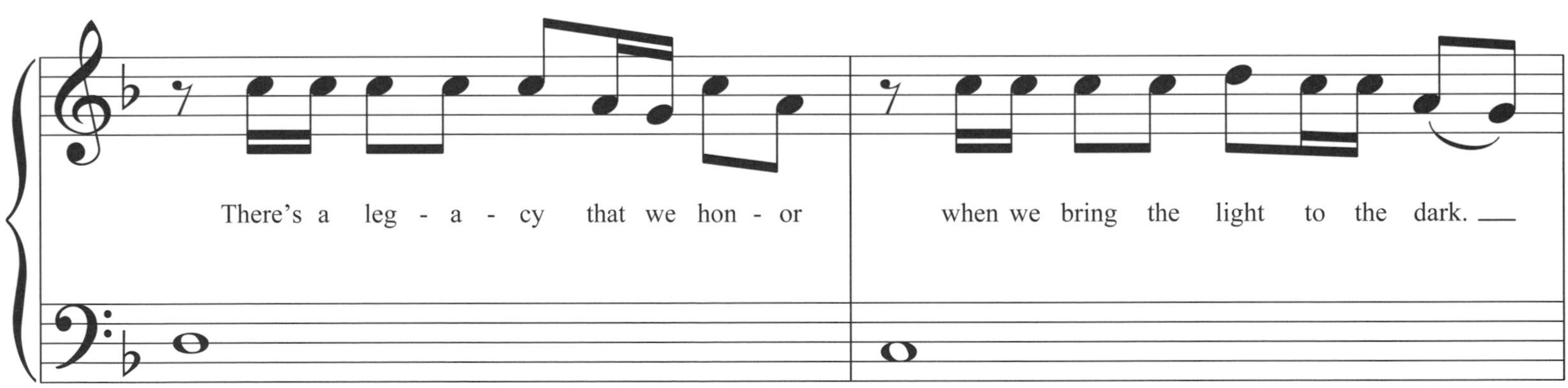
There's a leg - a - cy that we hon - or when we bring the light to the dark.

4
5
What - ev - er brings us to - geth - er can nev - er tear us a - part.

4
1
We be - come strong - er than ev - er
when we just trust.

When we just trust.

When we just trust.
When we just trust.

To Coda
(We'll lead the way.)

Ah,
ah,
ah,
ah,
ah.

1
Tak - ing the first step, I see you as my - self.

Noth - ing we can't do.
Put the past be - hind,

D.S. al Coda
2
learn from life this time. We can start brand new.

CODA

Ku - man - dra, Ku - man - dra,
Ku - man - dra, Ku - man - dra,

3
Ku - man - dra, Ku - man - dra,
Ku - man - dra, Ku - man - dra.
Ah,
ah,

ah,
ah,
ah,
ah,

ah,
ah,
ah,
ah,
ah.
5

POW! POW! POW! - MR. INCREDIBLE'S THEME

from INCREDIBLES 2

Music and Lyrics by
MICHAEL GIACCHINO

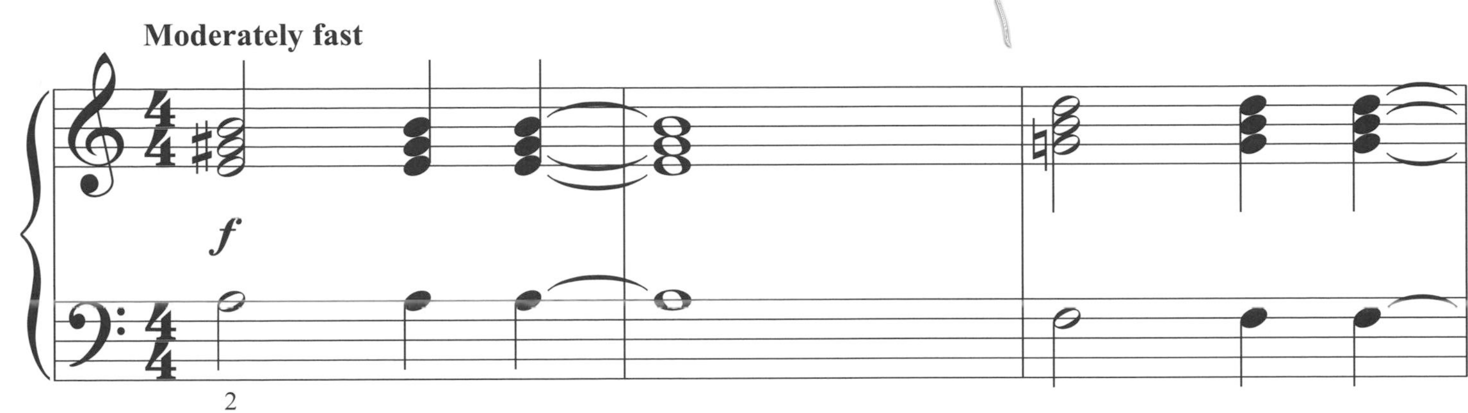

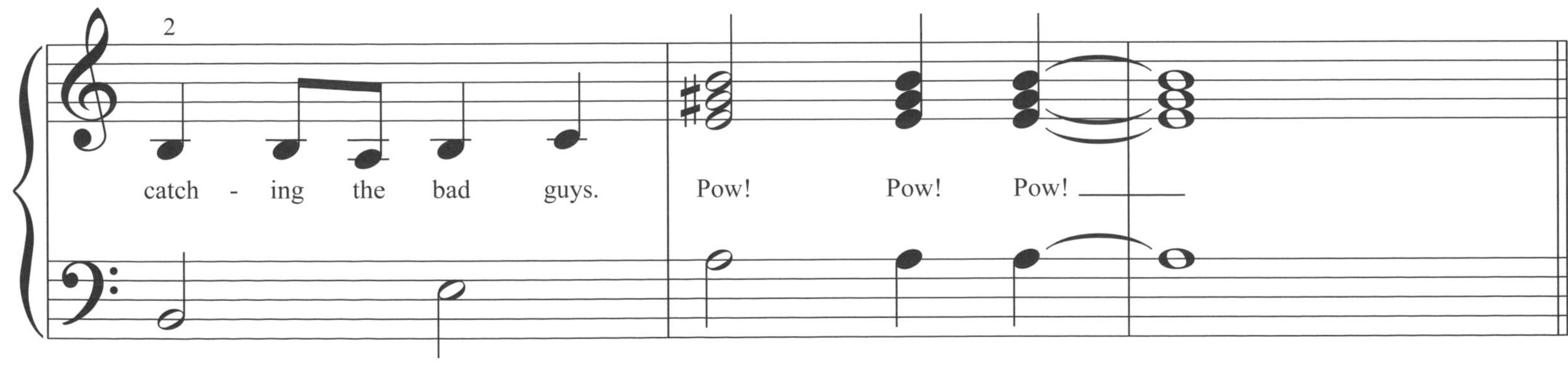

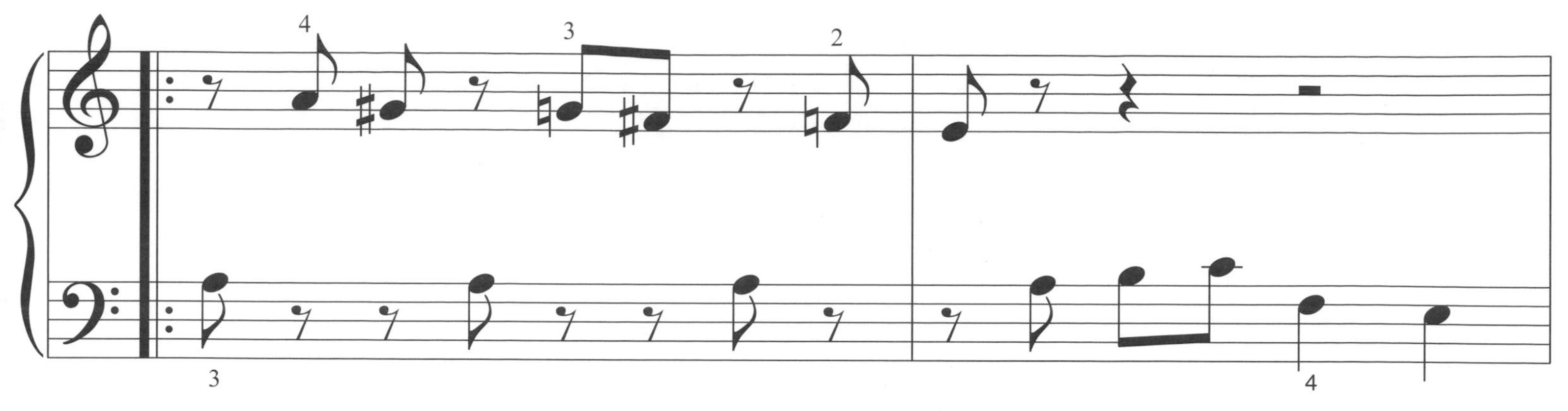
4
3
2
3
4

3

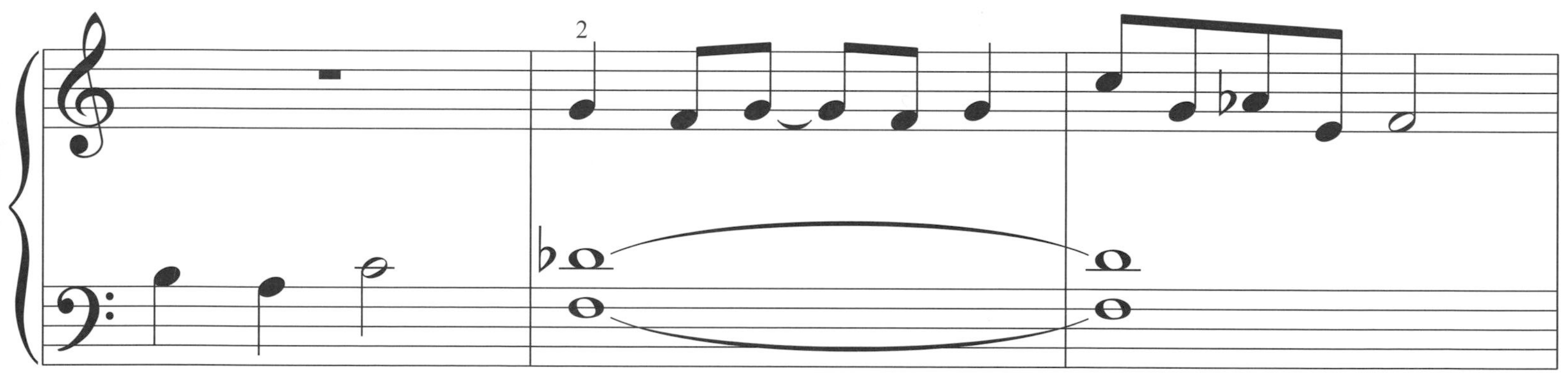
2

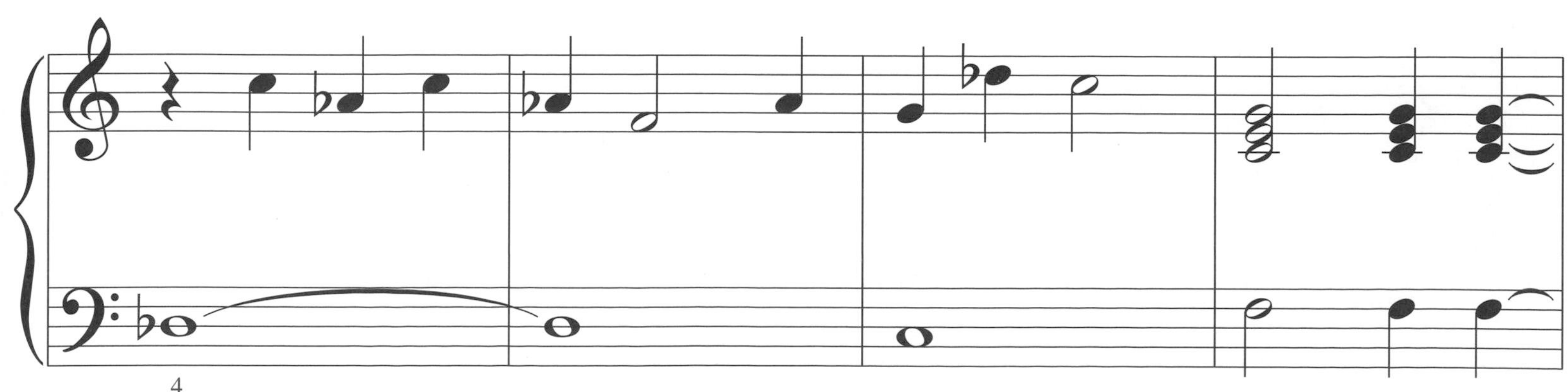
4

Mis - ter In - cred - i - ble, In -
cred - i - ble, In - cred - i - ble,
catch - ing the bad guys.
Pow! Pow! Pow! Pow! Pow!

LOST IN THE WOODS

from FROZEN 2

Music and Lyrics by KRISTEN ANDERSON-LOPEZ
and ROBERT LOPEZ

Moderately, in 2

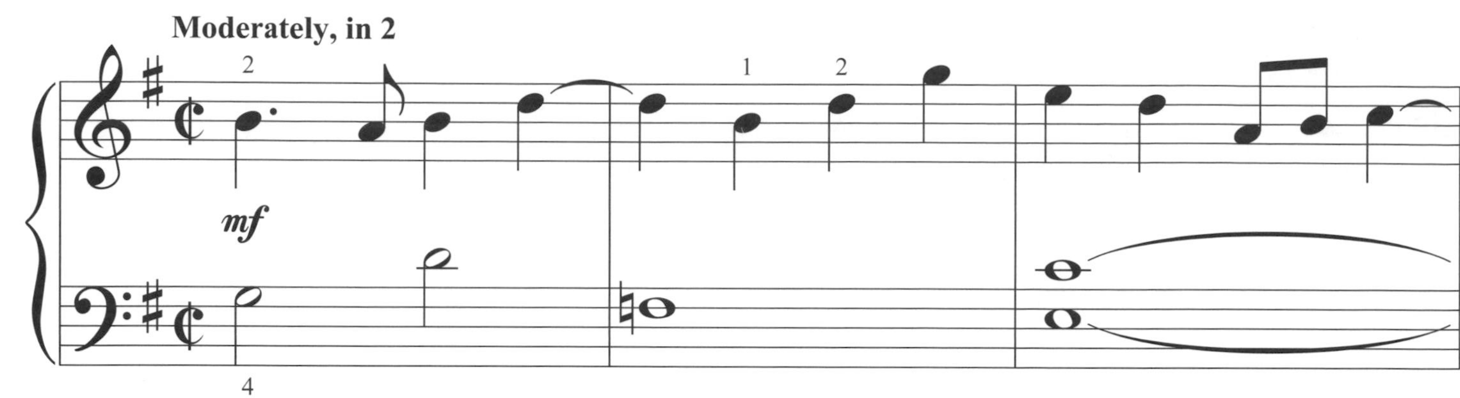

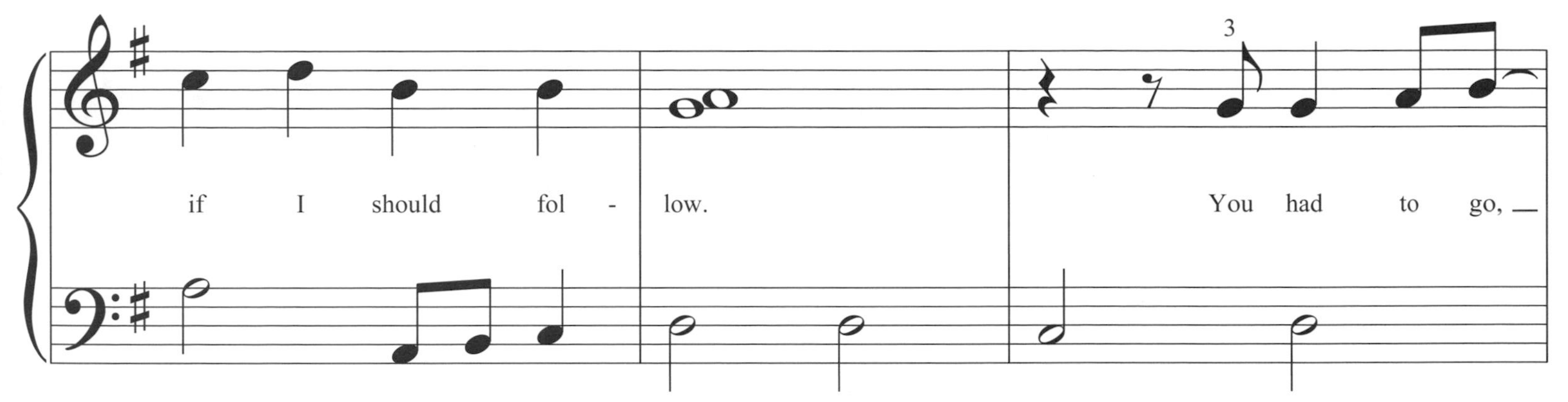
3
if I should fol - low.
You had to go,

3
and of course it's al - ways
3

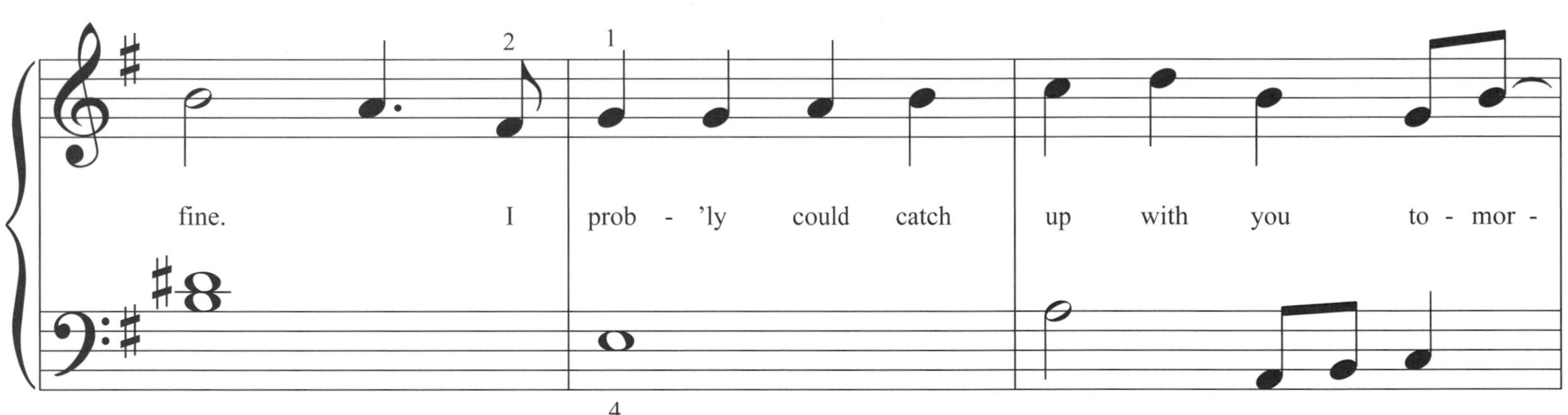
2
1
fine. I prob - 'ly could catch up with you to - mor -
4

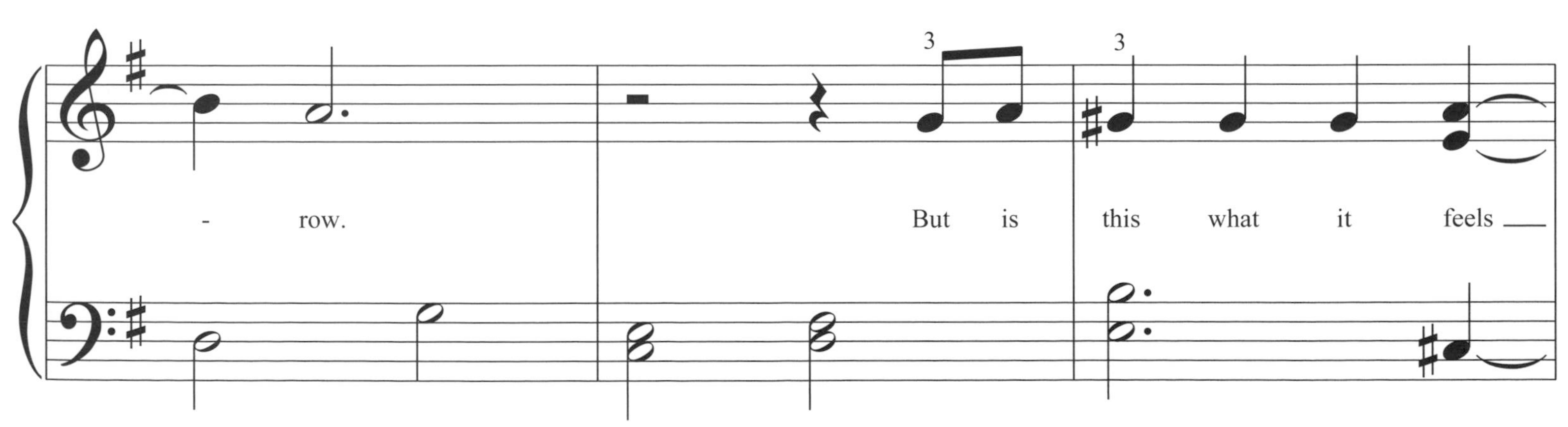
3
3
- row. But is this what it feels

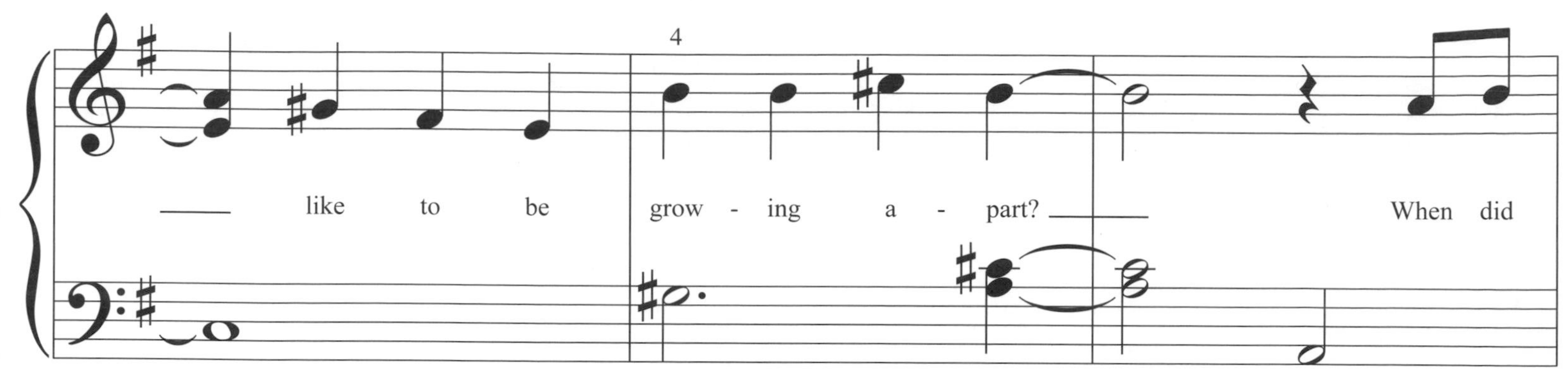
4
like to be grow - ing a - part? When did

4
4
3
I be - come the one who's al - ways chas - ing your heart?

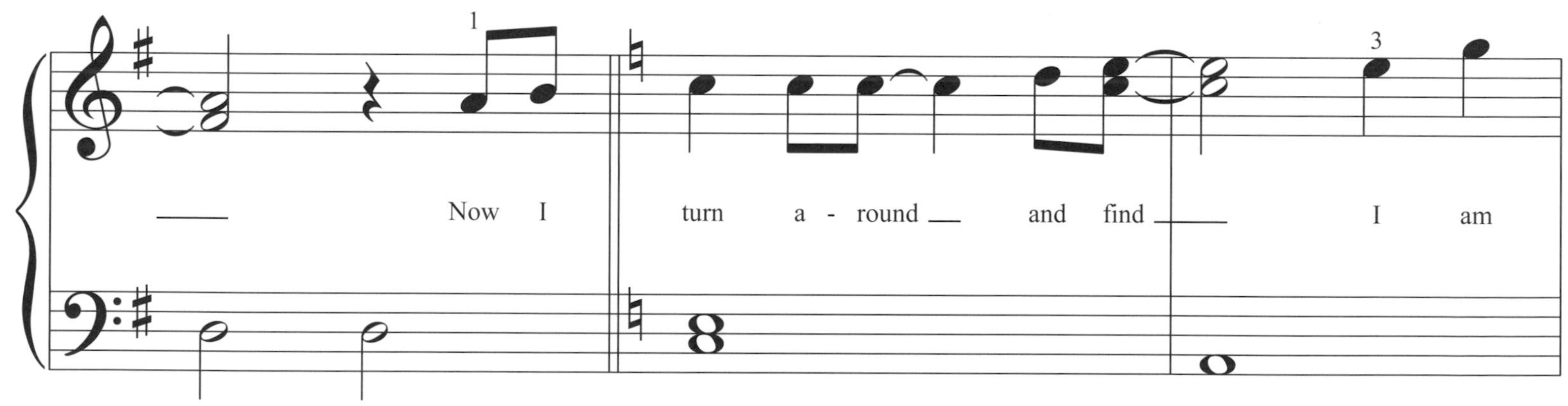
1
3
Now I turn a - round and find I am

5
2
lost in the woods. North is south, right is left
2

when you're gone.
I'm the one who sees you home,

but now I'm lost in the woods,
and I don't know what

path you are on.
I'm lost in the woods.

Up 'til now,

the next step was a ques - tion of how;

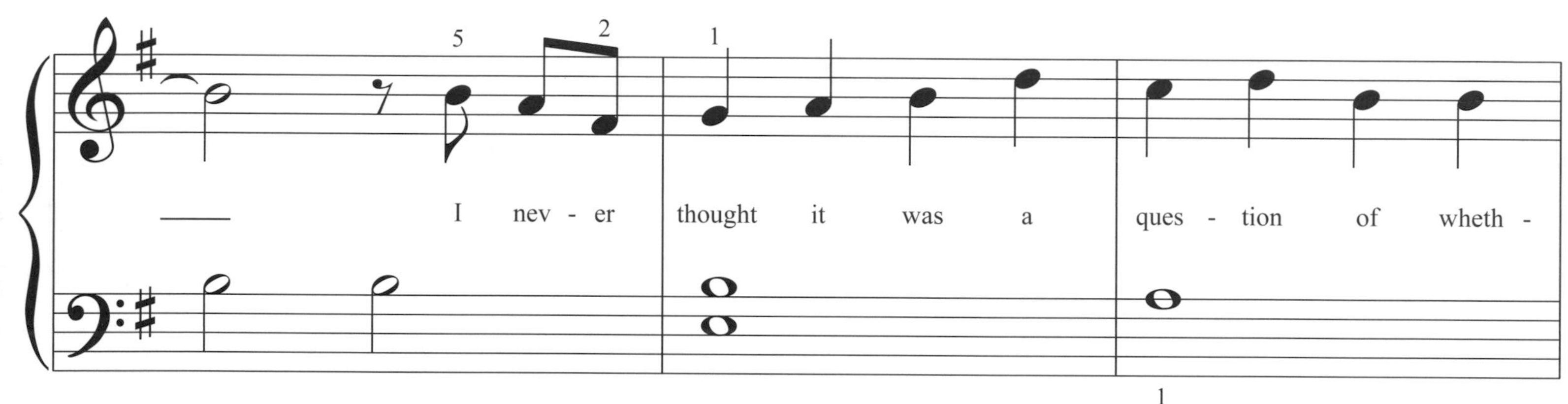

5 2 1
I nev - er thought it was a ques - tion of wheth -
1

er. Who am I if
4 4

I'm not your guy? Where am I if

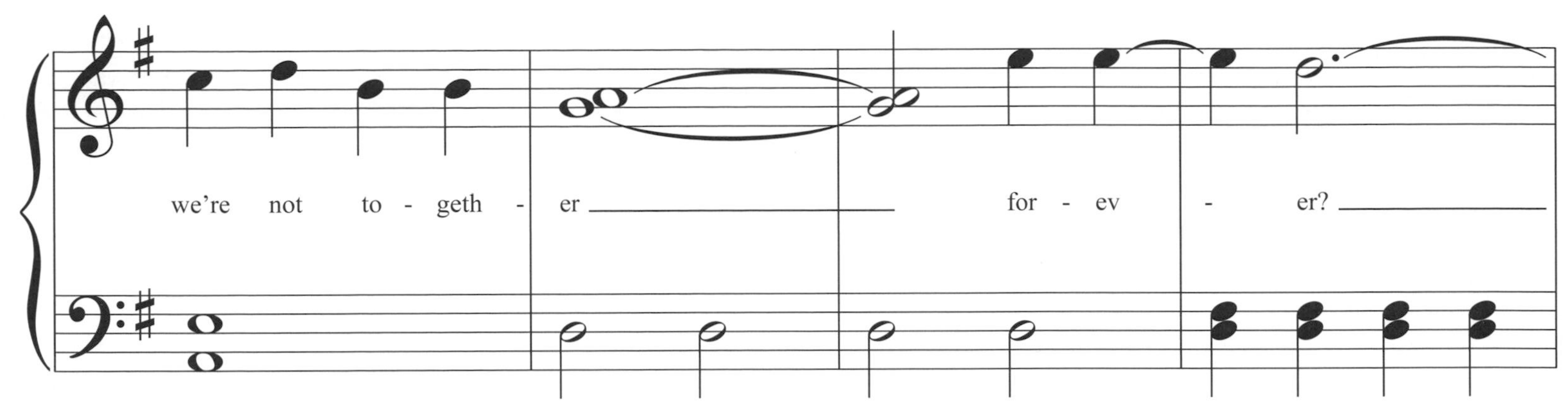
we're not to - geth - er
for - ev - er?

Now I
know you're my true North,
'cause I am
1

lost in the woods.
Up is down,
day is night
3
2
3

when you're not
there.
Oh,

1
you're my on - ly
land - mark, so I'm
lost in the woods, _
8

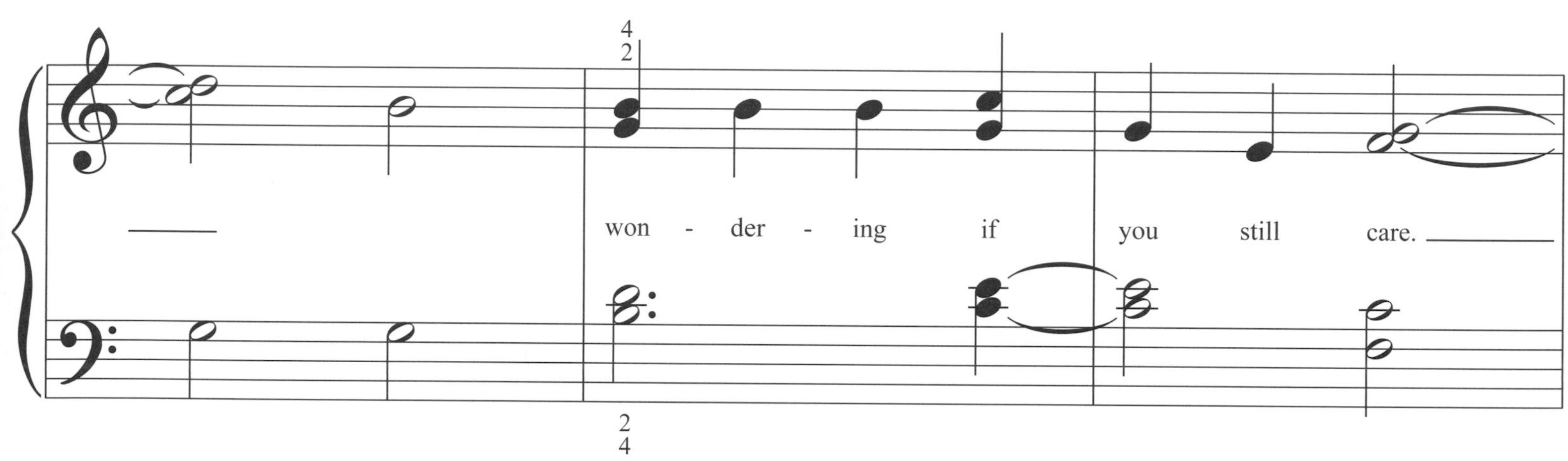
4
2
won - der - ing if
you still care. _
2
4

But I'll wait _
3

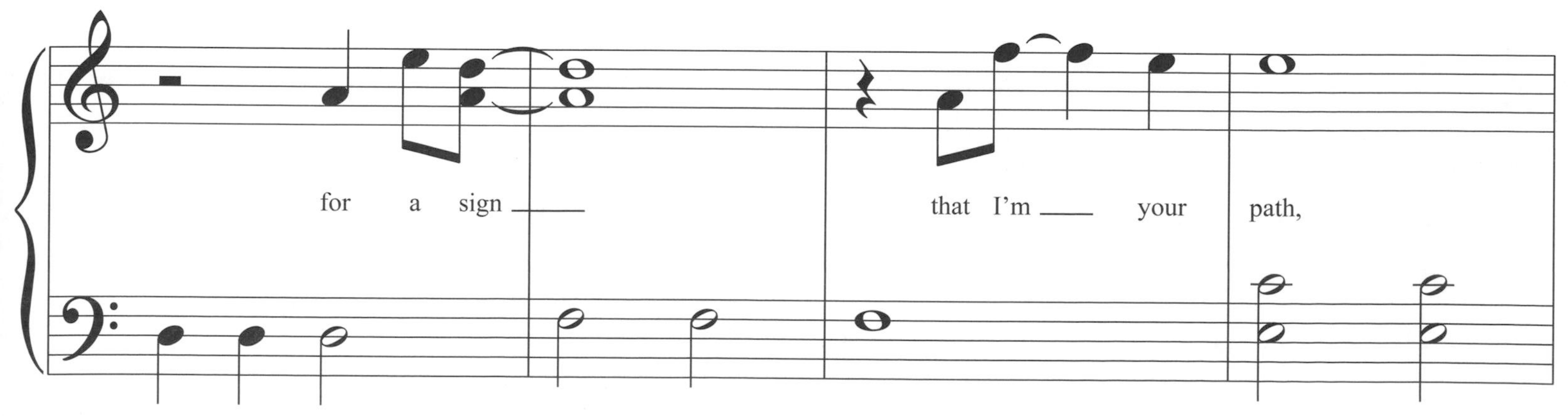
for a sign _
that I'm _ your
path,

3
1
'cause you ___ are
mine.
Un - til
then,
I'm
2

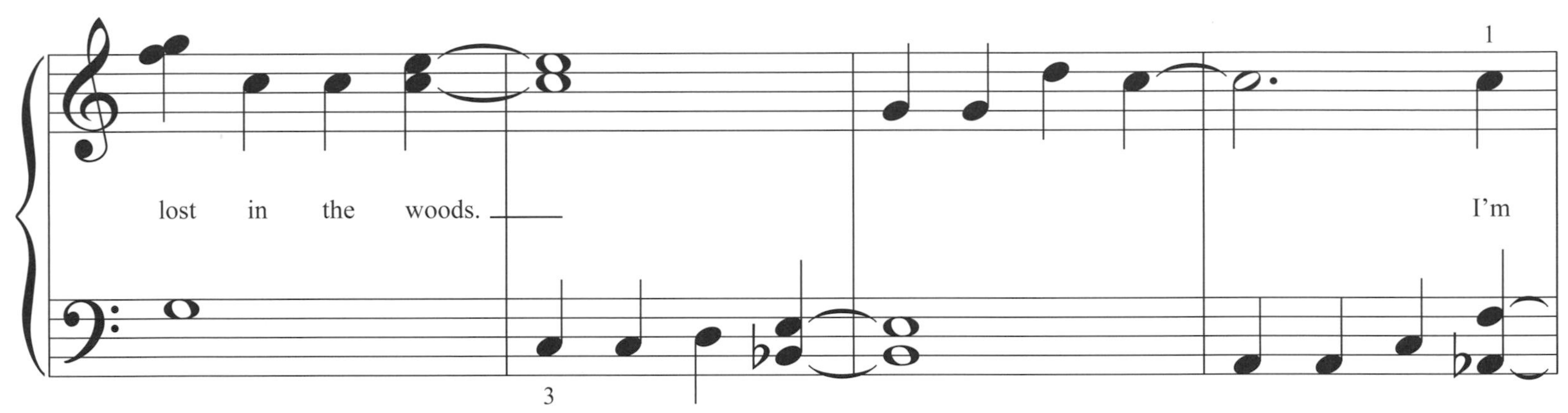
1
lost in the woods. ___
I'm
3

3
lost in the woods. ___
I'm
3

1
lost in the woods.

LOYAL BRAVE TRUE

from MULAN 2020

Written by JAMIE HARTMAN,
BILLY CRABTREE, ROSI GOLAN
and HARRY GREGSON-WILLIAMS

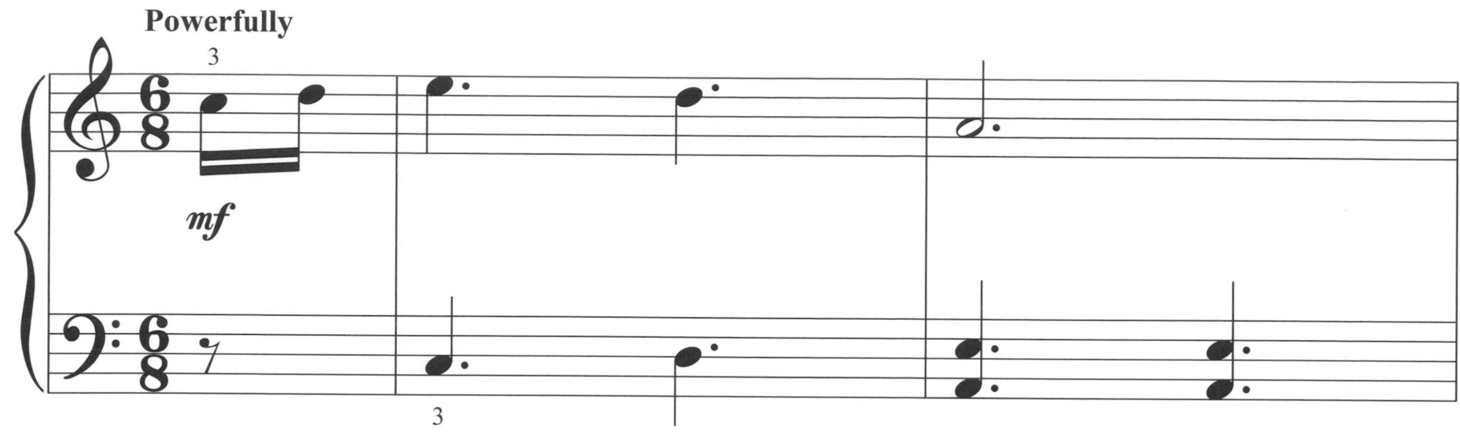

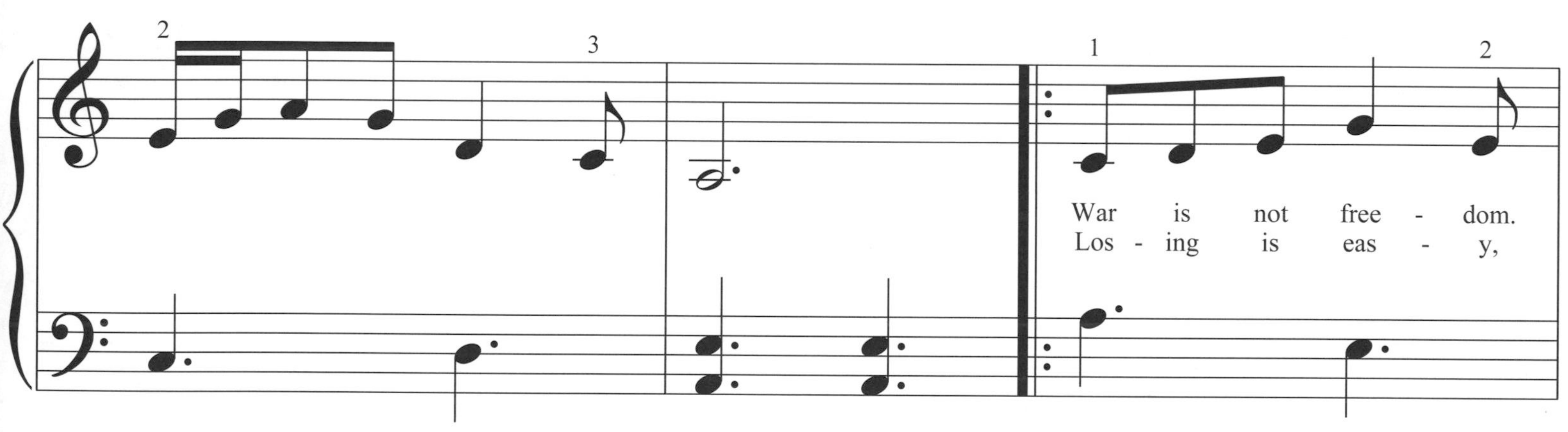

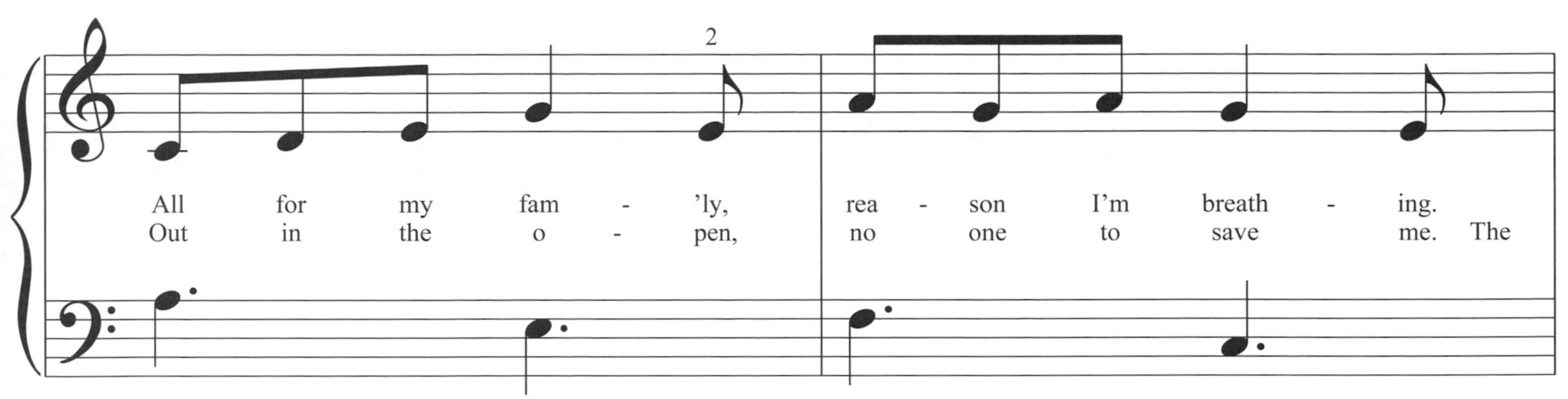
2
All for my fam - 'ly,
Out in the o - pen,
rea - son I'm breath - ing.
no one to save me. The

1
Ev - er - y - thing to lose.
kind - est of whis - pers are cruel.
Should I ask my - self in the
4

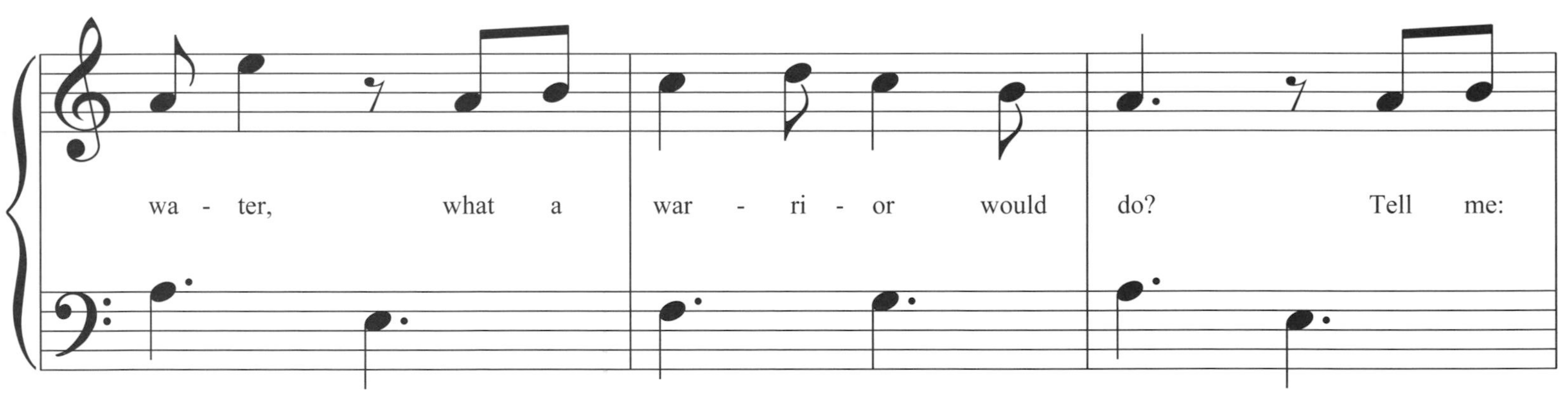
wa - ter, what a war - ri - or would do? Tell me:

un - der - neath my ar - mor, am I loy - al, brave and
3

1.

true? Am I loy - al, brave and true? ___

2.

true? ___ Cold is the morn - ing, warm is the

strong - er or will I be weak when you're not with me?

Who am I with - out my ar - mor, stand - ing
mp

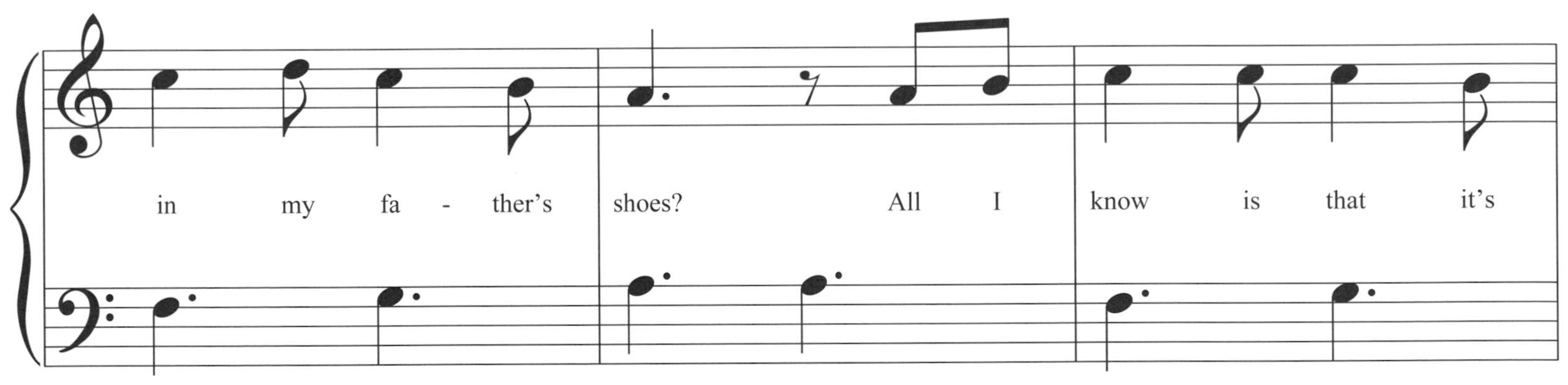
in my fa - ther's shoes? All I know is that it's

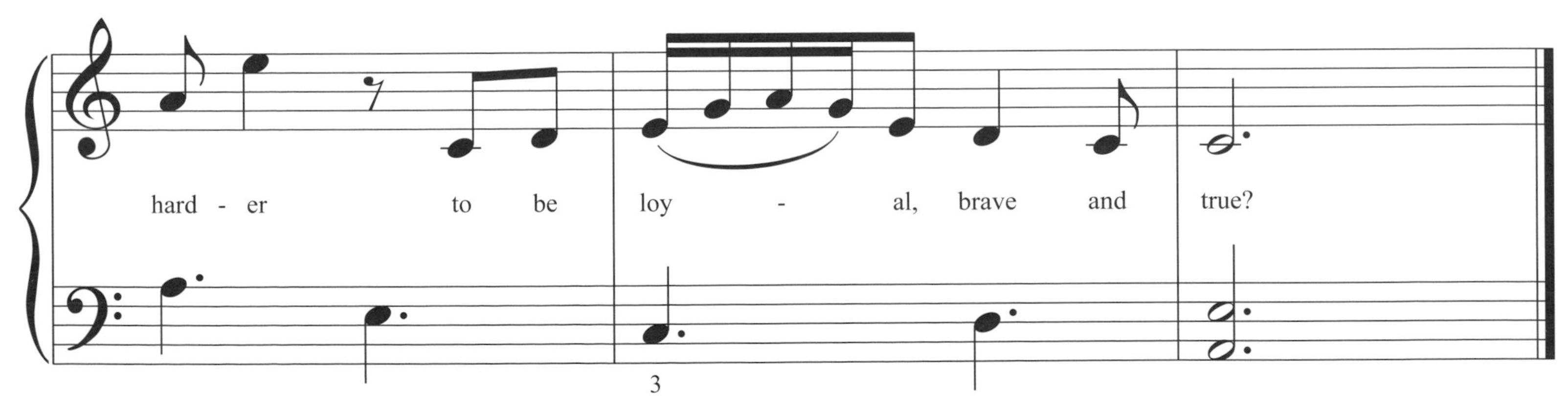
hard - er to be loy - al, brave and true?
3

REMEMBER ME

(Ernesto de la Cruz)
from COCO

Music and Lyrics by KRISTEN ANDERSON-LOPEZ
and ROBERT LOPEZ

Moderately fast

2
3
night we are a - part. Re - mem - ber me though I have to tra - vel far. Re - mem - ber

3
me each time you hear a sad gui - tar. Know that I'm with you the on - ly

5
1
way that I can be. Un - til you're in my arms a - gain, re - mem - ber
1
3

1
me.

4
Re - mem - ber

2
3
3
me, though I
have to say good - bye. Re - mem - ber
me, don't

let it make you cry. For
e - ven if I'm far a - way, I
hold you in my heart. I
2

4
sing a se - cret song to you each night we are a - part. Re - mem - ber me though I

3
have to tra - vel far. Re - mem - ber me each time you hear a sad gui - tar.

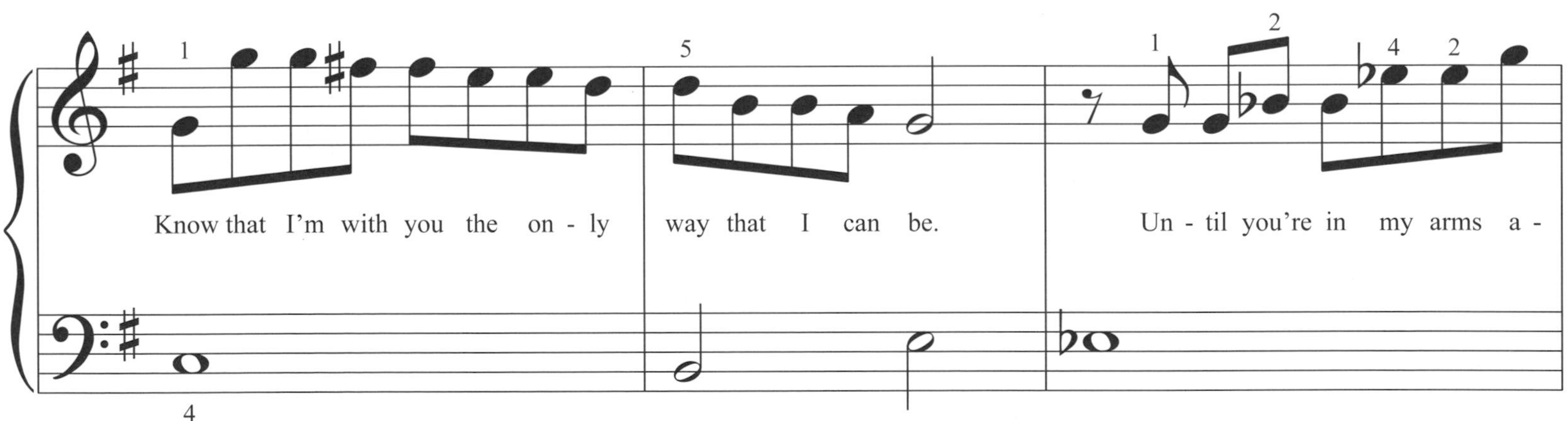
1 5 1 2 4 2
Know that I'm with you the on - ly way that I can be. Un - til you're in my arms a -
4

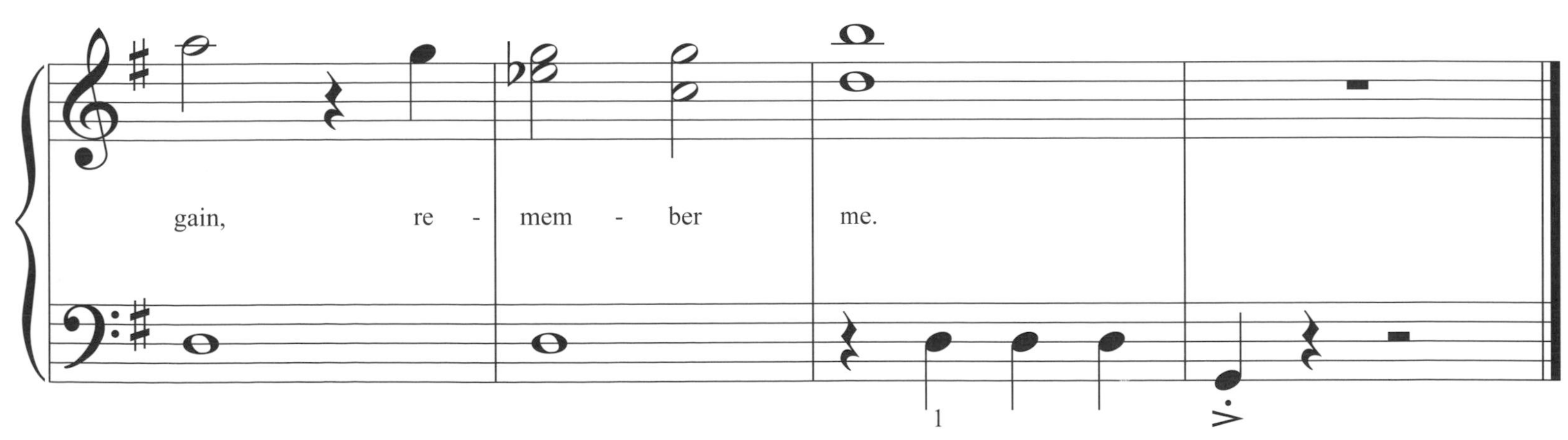
gain, re - mem - ber me.
1

SOME THINGS NEVER CHANGE

from FROZEN 2

Music and Lyrics by KRISTEN ANDERSON-LOPEZ
and ROBERT LOPEZ

Rhythmically

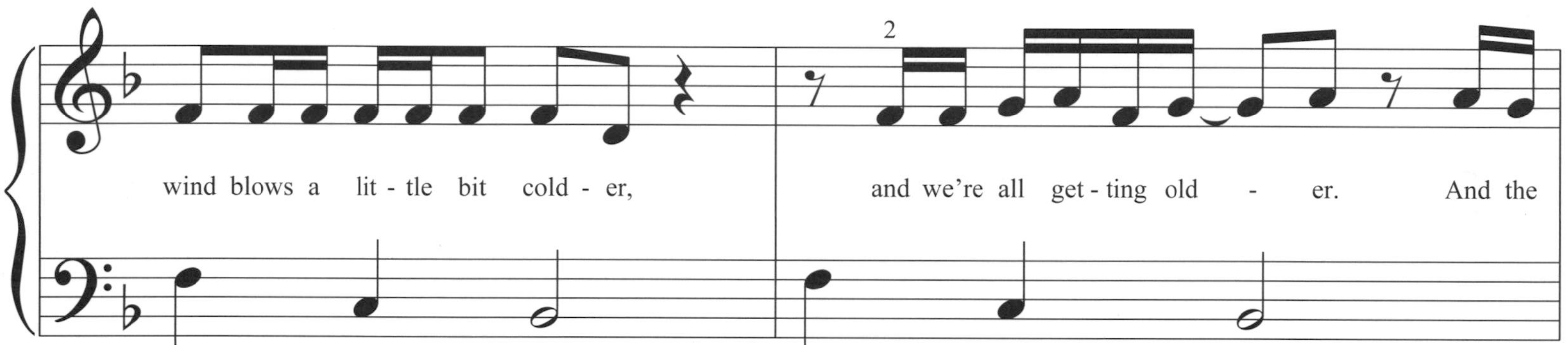

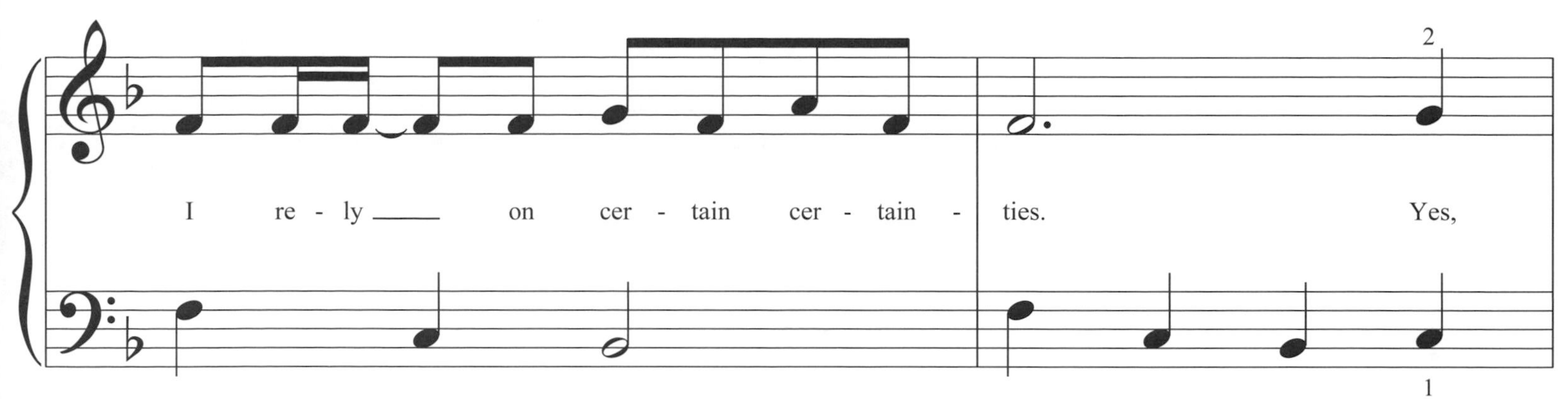
2
I re - ly ___ on cer - tain cer - tain - ties. Yes,
1

Swing 16ths
5
2
some things nev - er change, ___
2
like the feel of your hand in mine. ___

5
Some things stay the same, ___
2
1
like how we get a - long ___ just fine. Like an

old stone wall that - 'll nev - er fall,
3
some things are al - ways true! ___
3
3

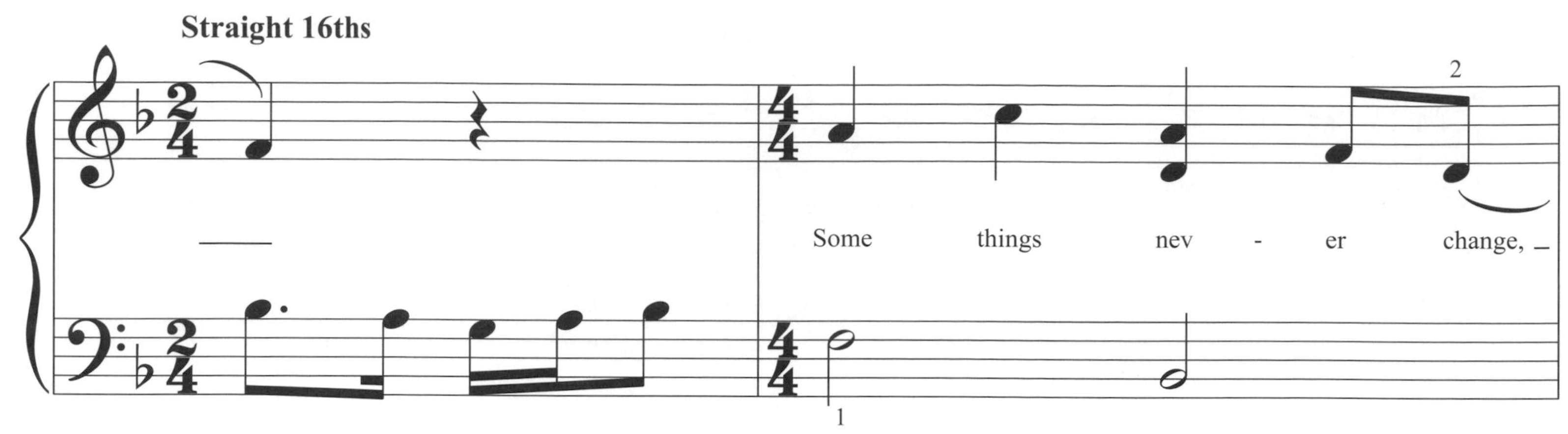
Straight 16ths
2
Some things nev - er change,
1

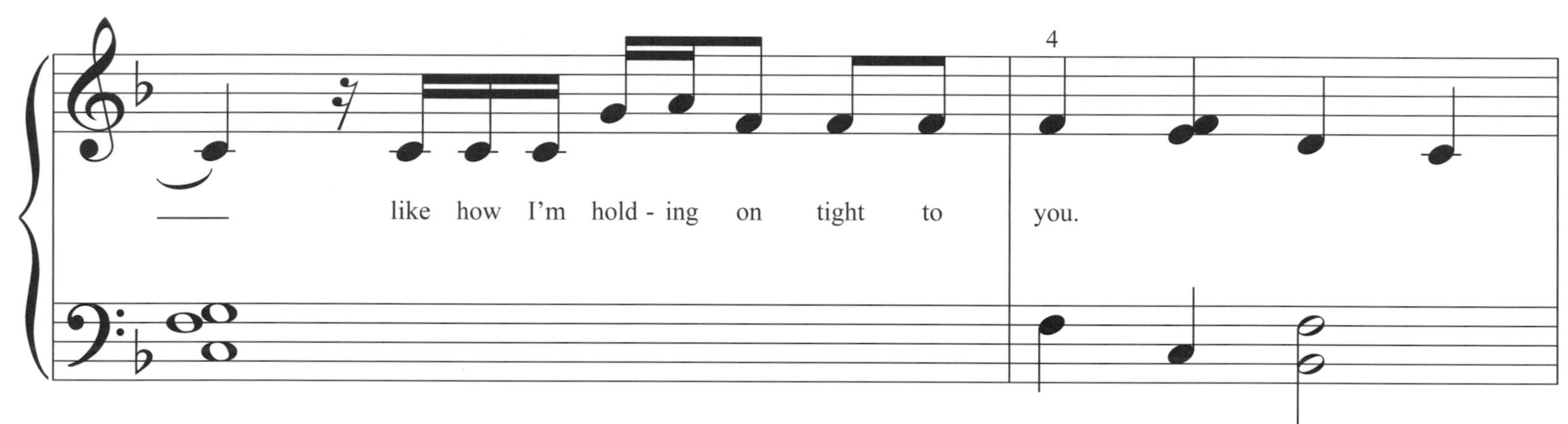
4
like how I'm hold - ing on tight to you.

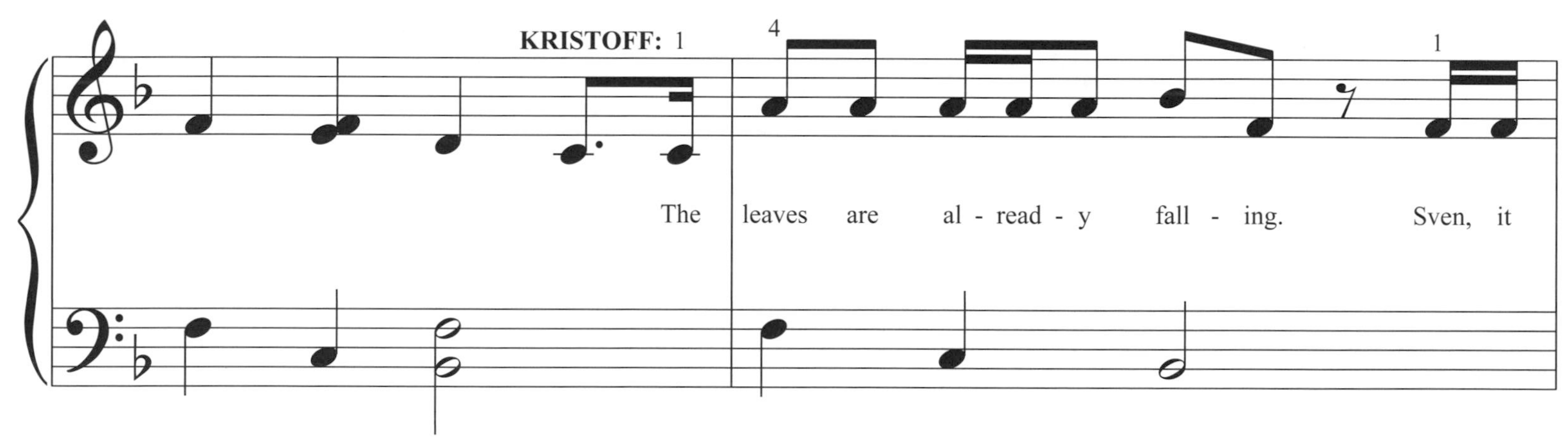
KRISTOFF: 1
4
1
The leaves are al - read - y fall - ing. Sven, it

4
SVEN:
feels like the fu - ture is call - ing! Are you tell - ing me to - night you're gon - na get down on one

KRISTOFF:
OLAF:
knee? Yeah, but I'm real - ly bad at plan-ning these things out, like

SVEN:
can - dle-light and pull - ing of rings out. May - be you should leave all the ro - man - tic stuff to

Swing 16ths
KRISTOFF:
me. Yeah, some things nev - er change,

like the love that I feel for her. Some things stay the same,

like how rein-deers are eas - i - er. But if I com - mit and I go for it, I'll

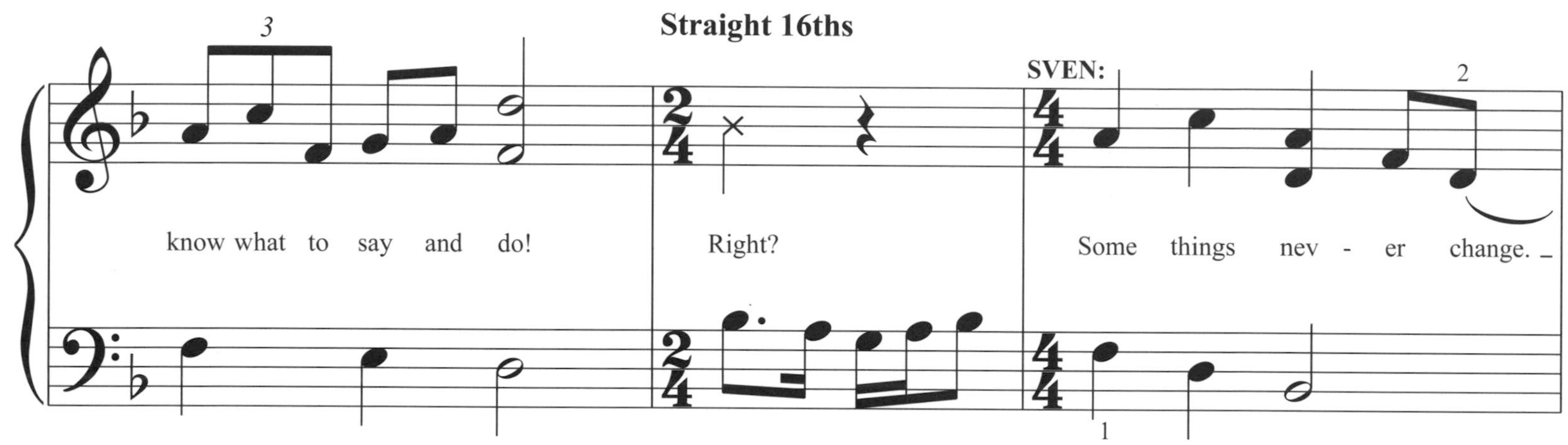
Straight 16ths
SVEN:
know what to say and do! Right? Some things nev - er change.

KRISTOFF:
Sven, the pres-sure is all on you.

ELSA:
The winds are rest-less; could that be why I'm hear-ing this call? Is some-thing com - ing? I'm

1
2
not sure I want things to change at
all. These days are pre - cious, can't

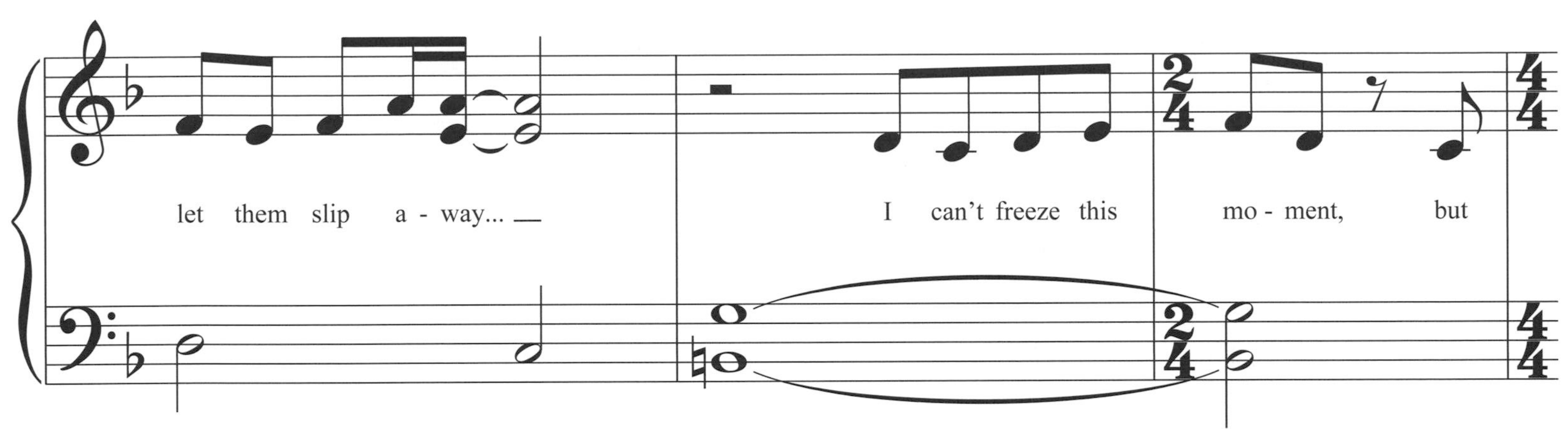
let them slip a - way...
I can't freeze this
mo - ment, but

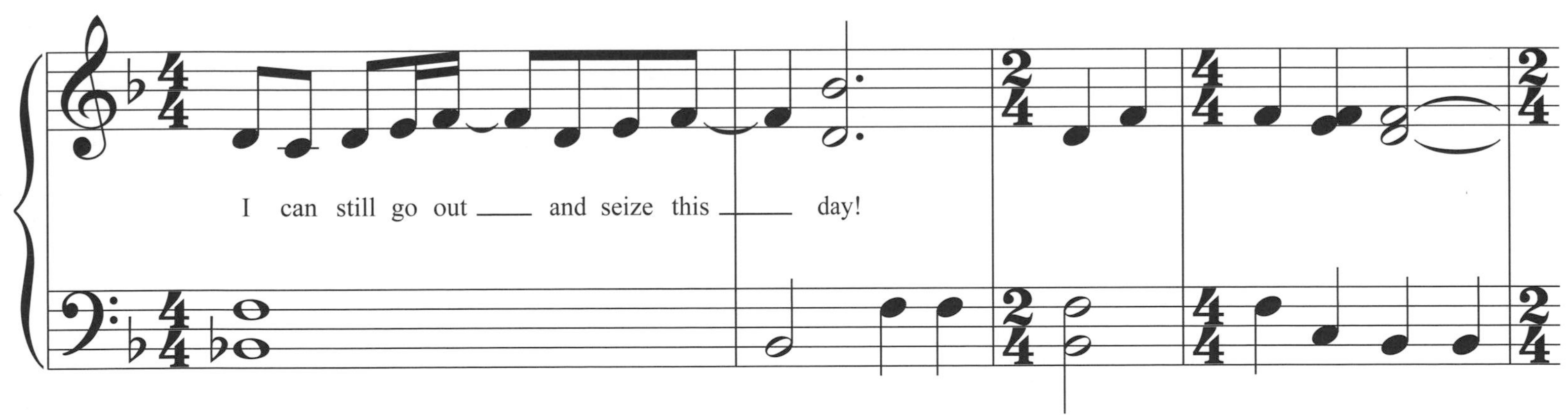
I can still go out and seize this
day!

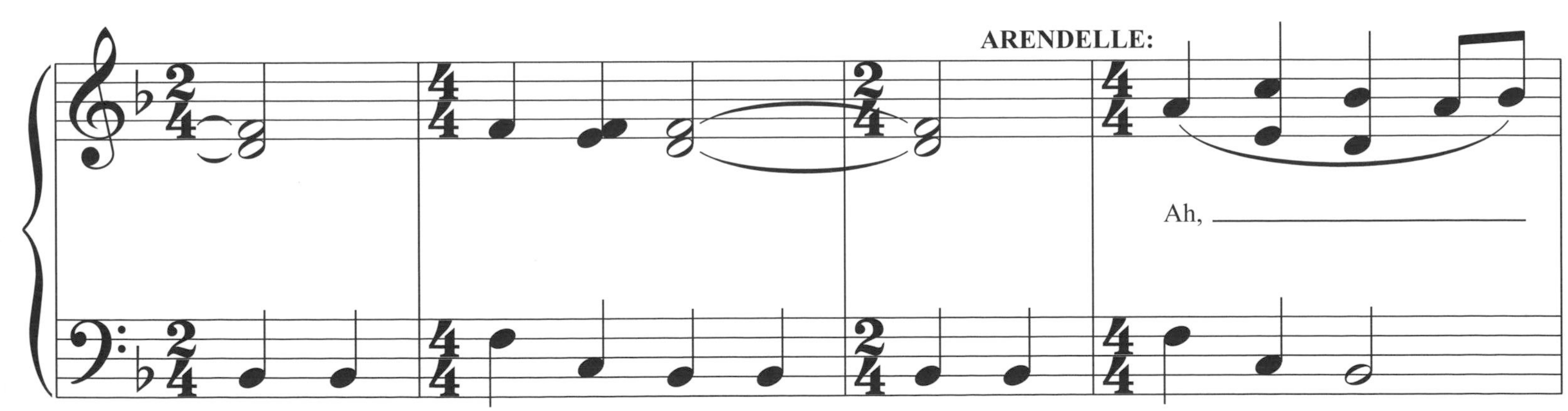
ARENDELLE:
Ah,

OLAF:
oh. The
wind blows a lit - tle bit cold - er. And you

ANNA:
2
all look a lit - tle bit old - er! It's
time to count our bless-ings be - neath an au - tumn

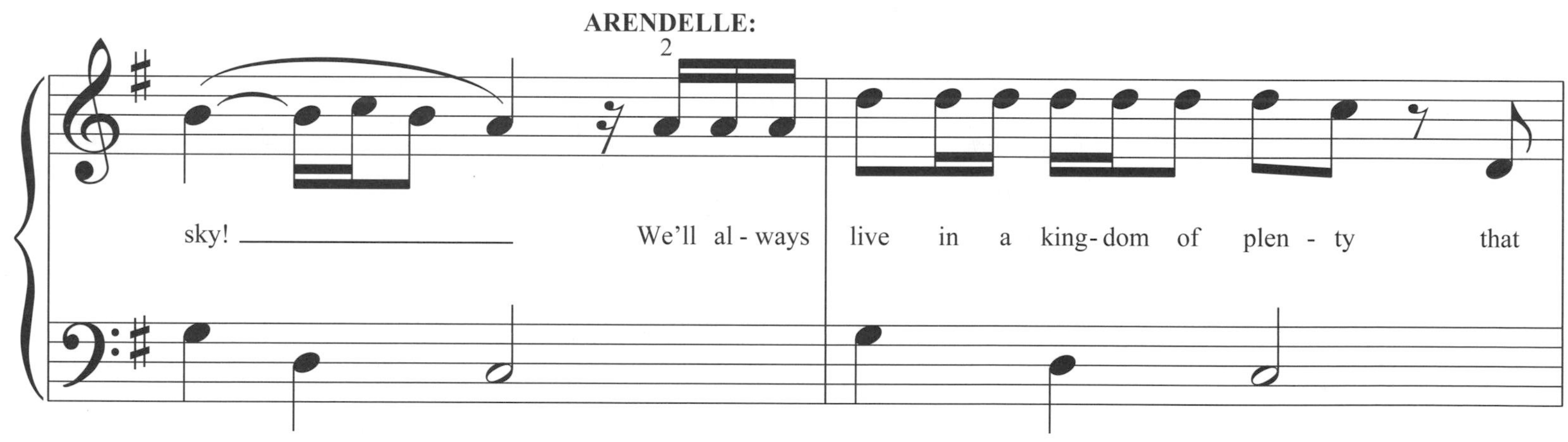
ARENDELLE:
2
sky! We'll al - ways
live in a king-dom of plen - ty that

3
ELSA:
stands for the good of the man - y! And I
prom-ise you the flag of Ar - en-delle will al - ways

ANNA:
fly! Our flag will al - ways
ARENDELLE:
fly! Our flag will al - ways, our
flag will al - ways fly!
Swing 16ths
ALL:
Some things nev - er change;
turn a - round, and the time has flown.
Some things stay the same,
though the fu - ture re - mains un - known. May our
good luck last, may our past be past.

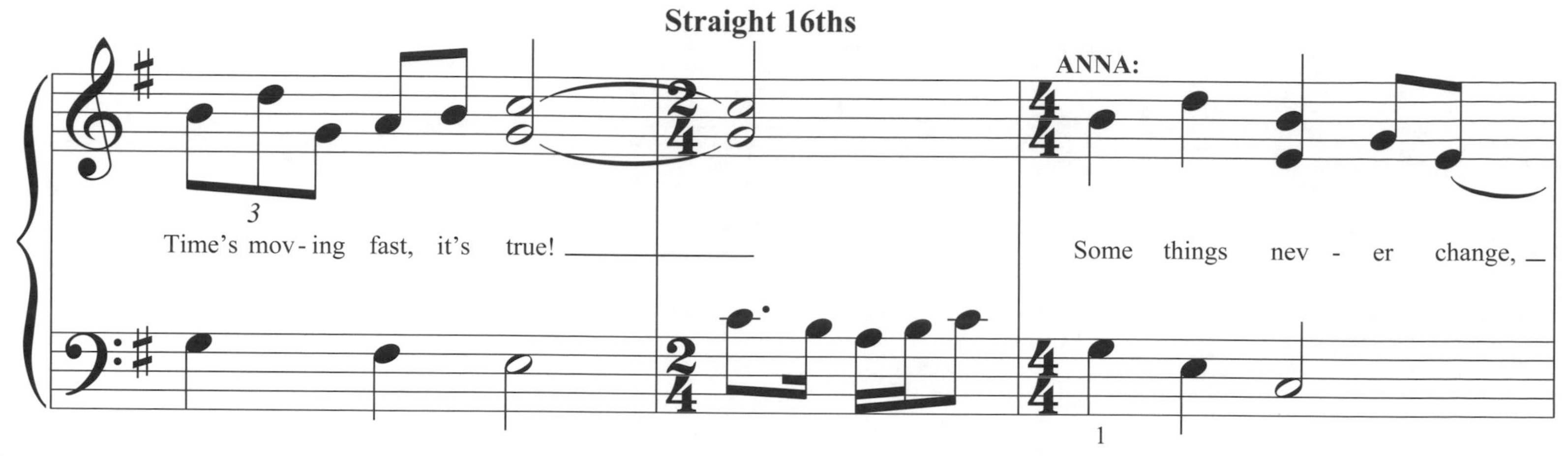
Straight 16ths
ANNA:
3
Time's mov - ing fast, it's true!
Some things nev - er change,
1
1

1
ELSA:
and I'm hold - ing on tight to
you...
Hold - ing on tight to...

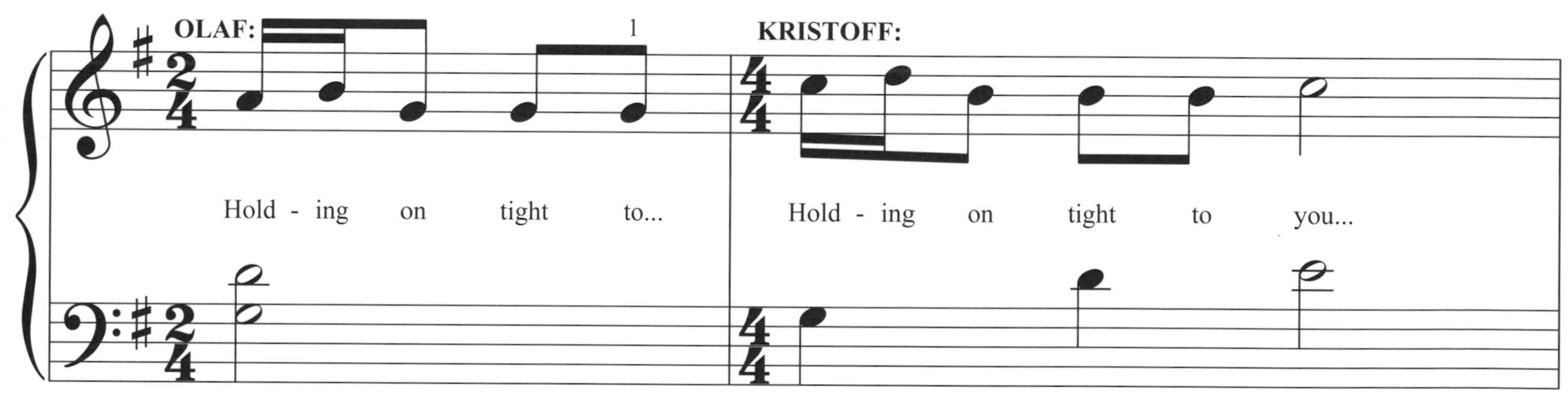
OLAF:
1
KRISTOFF:
Hold - ing on tight to...
Hold - ing on tight to you...

ANNA:
I'm hold - ing on tight to you.

WHEN WE'RE HUMAN

from THE PRINCESS AND THE FROG

Music and Lyrics by
RANDY NEWMAN

Moderately fast Dixieland

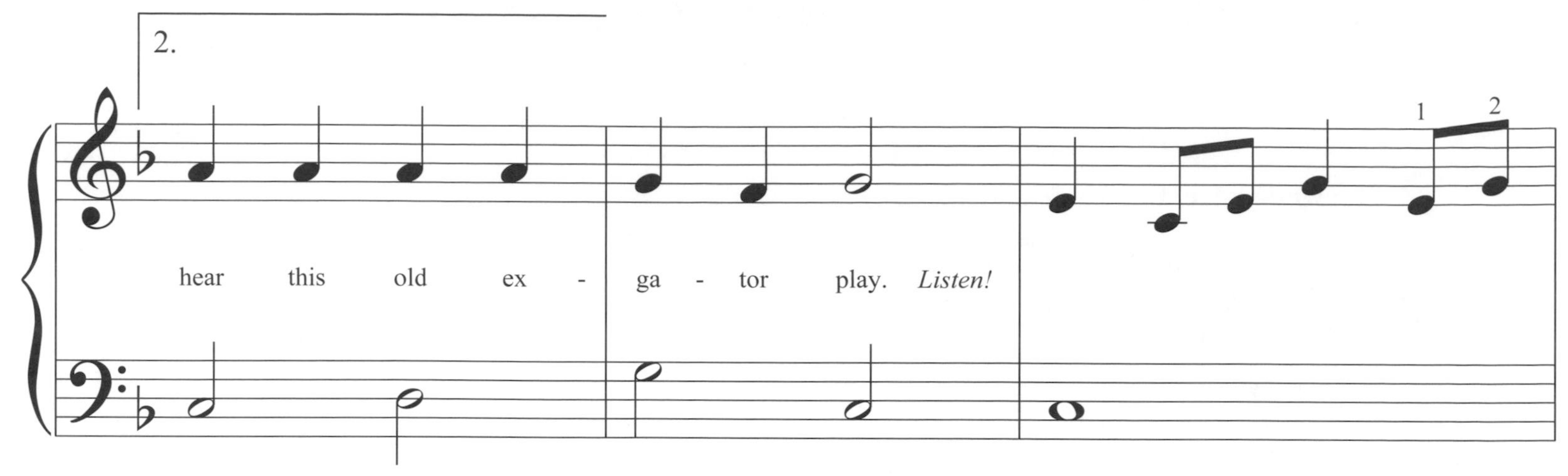
2.
1
2
hear this old ex - ga - tor play. Listen!

2

When I'm hu - man,

2
as I hope to be, I'm gon - na blow this horn 'til the

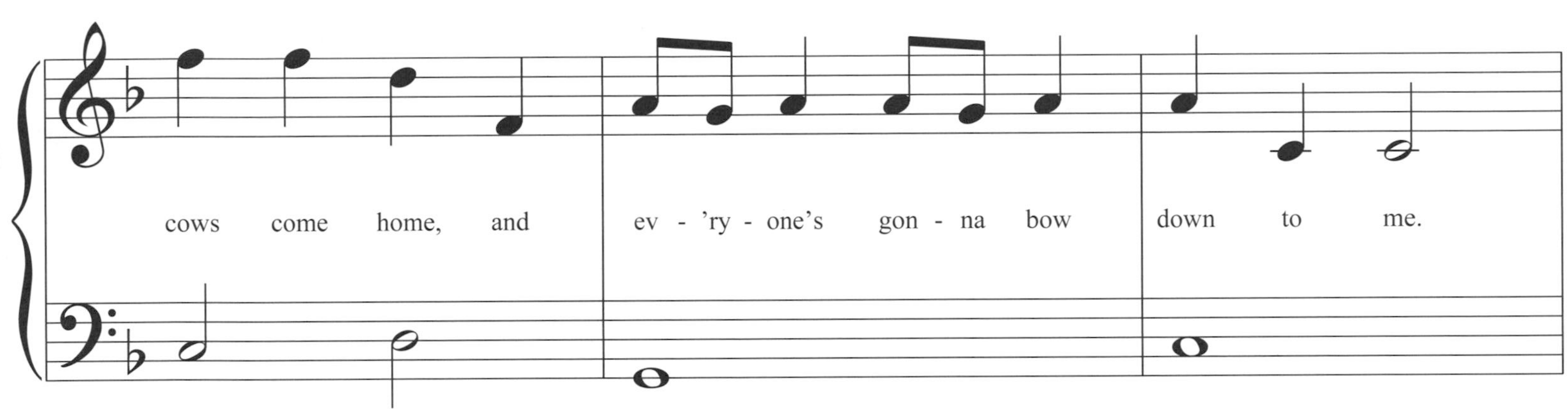
cows come home, and ev - 'ry - one's gon - na bow down to me.

PRINCE NAVEEN:
When I'm my - self a - gain, I want just the life I
5
5

had: a great big par - ty ev - 'ry night.

3
That seems just a - bout
right, eh, Lou - is?
Life is short; when you're
1

done, you're done; we're
on this earth to
have some fun. And

that's the way things
are.
When I'm
hu - man,

and I'm gon - na
2
be, I'm gon - na
tear it up like I

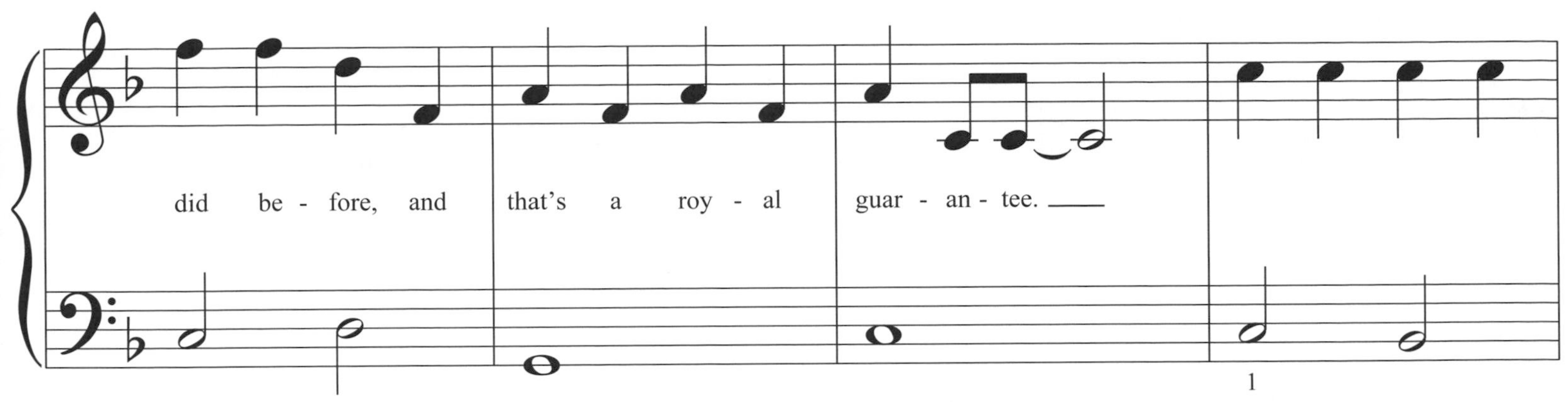
did be - fore, and that's a roy - al guar - an - tee.
1

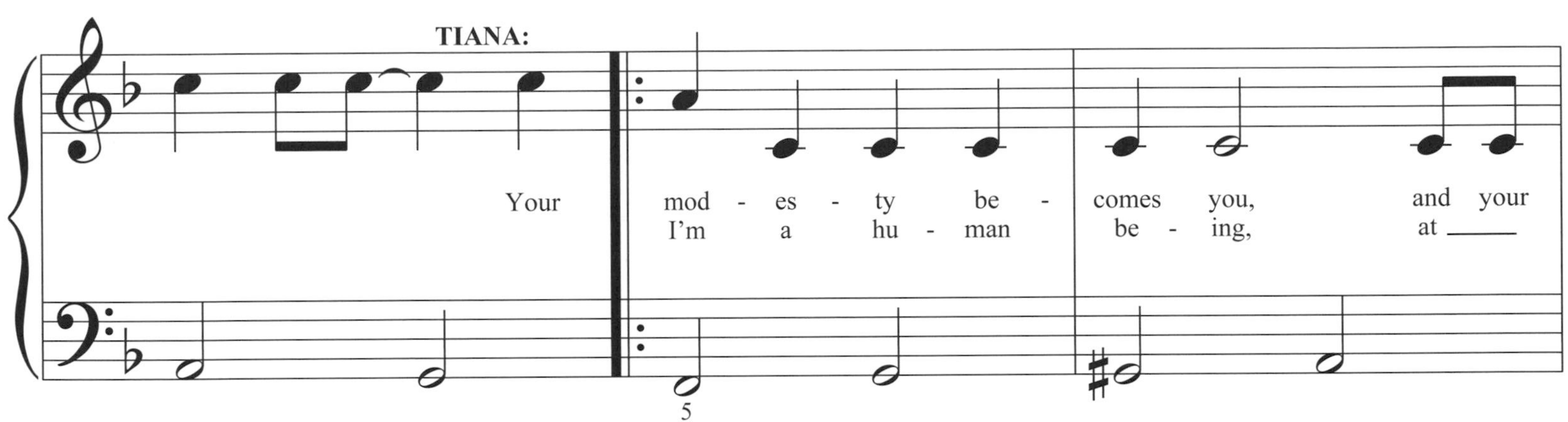
TIANA:
Your mod - es - ty be - comes you, and your
I'm a hu - man be - ing, at
5

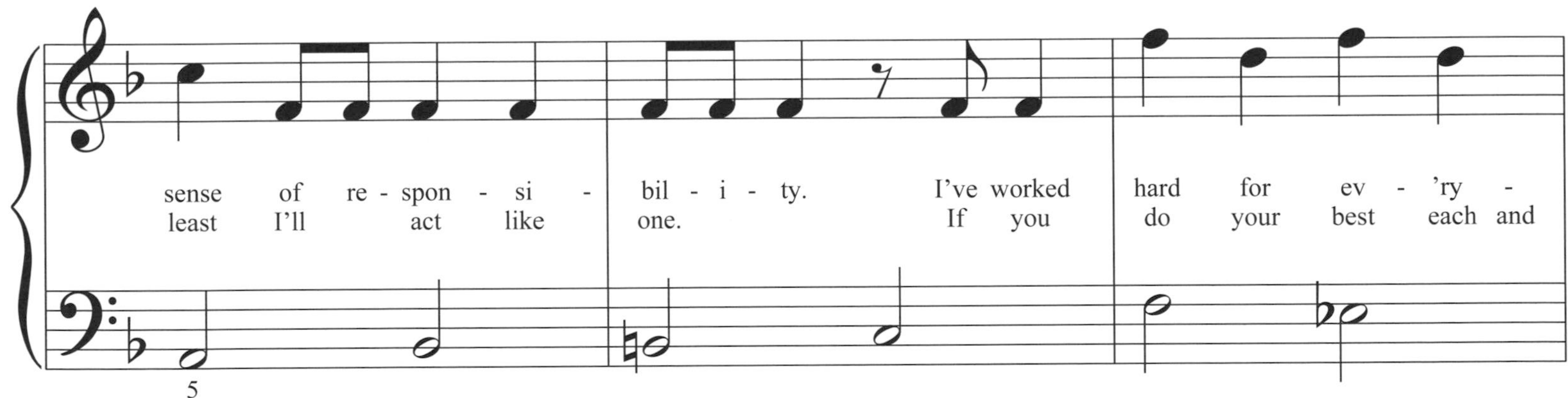
sense of re - spon - si - bil - i - ty. I've worked hard for ev - 'ry -
least I'll act like one. If you do your best each and
5

1.
5
thing I've got and that's the way it's sup - posed to be. When
ev - 'ry day,

2.
good things are sure to
come your way.
What you give is
1

what you get. My
dad - dy said that, and I'll
nev - er for - get. And

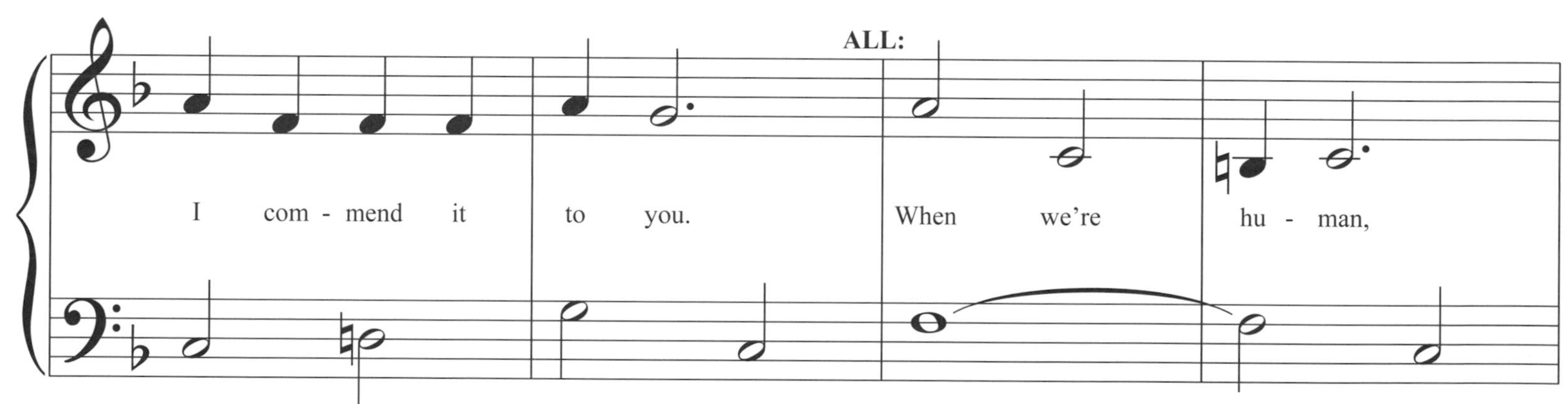
I com - mend it
to you.
ALL:
When we're
hu - man,

2
and we're gon - na
LOUIS:
be... I'm gon - na
blow my horn.

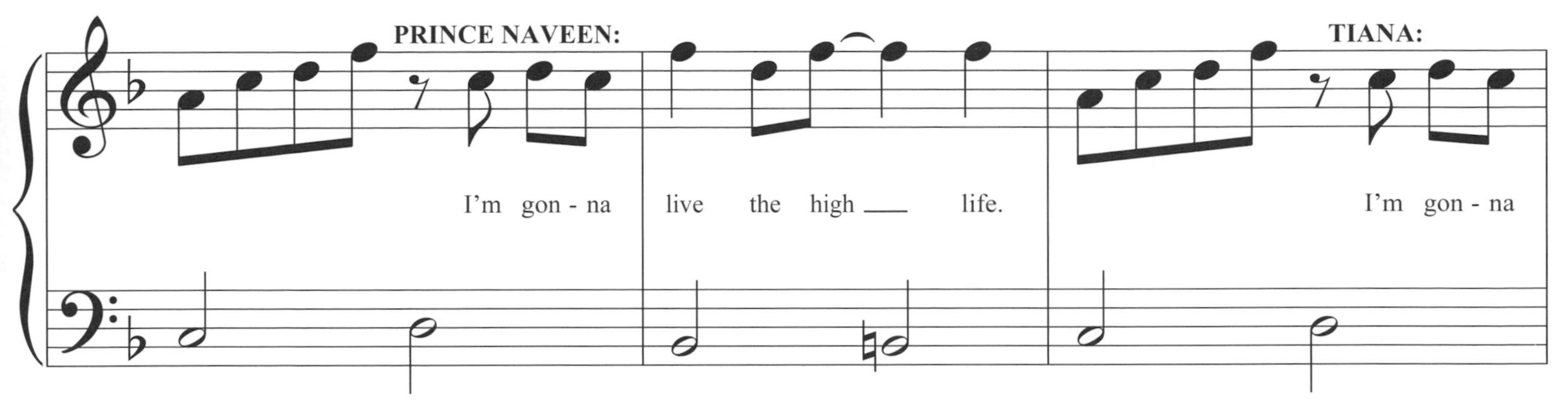
PRINCE NAVEEN:
TIANA:
I'm gon - na live the high ___ life. I'm gon - na

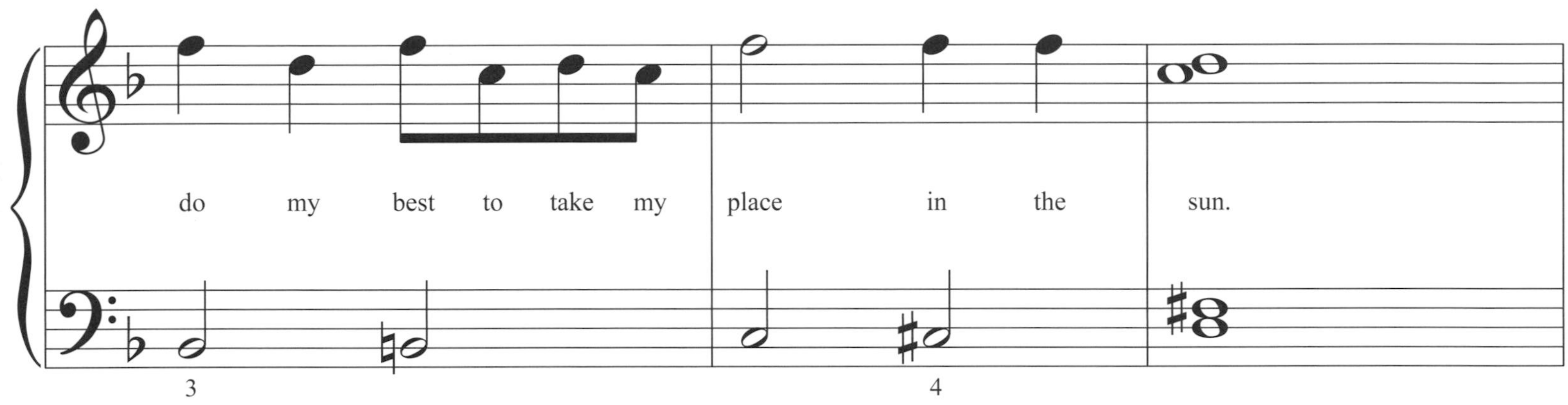
do my best to take my place in the sun.
3
4

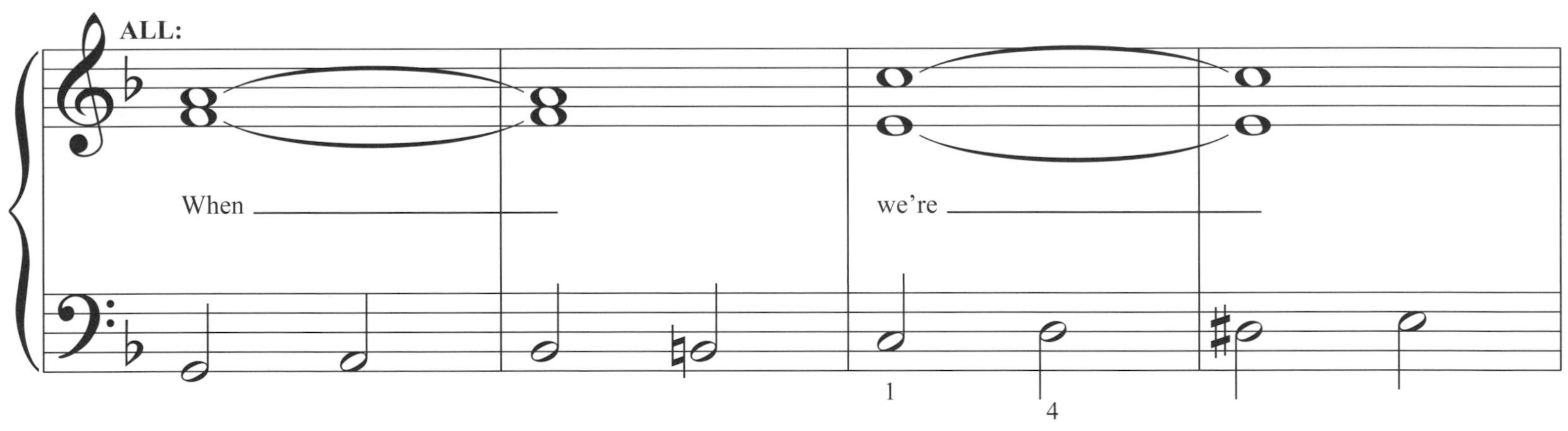
ALL:
When ___ we're ___
1
4

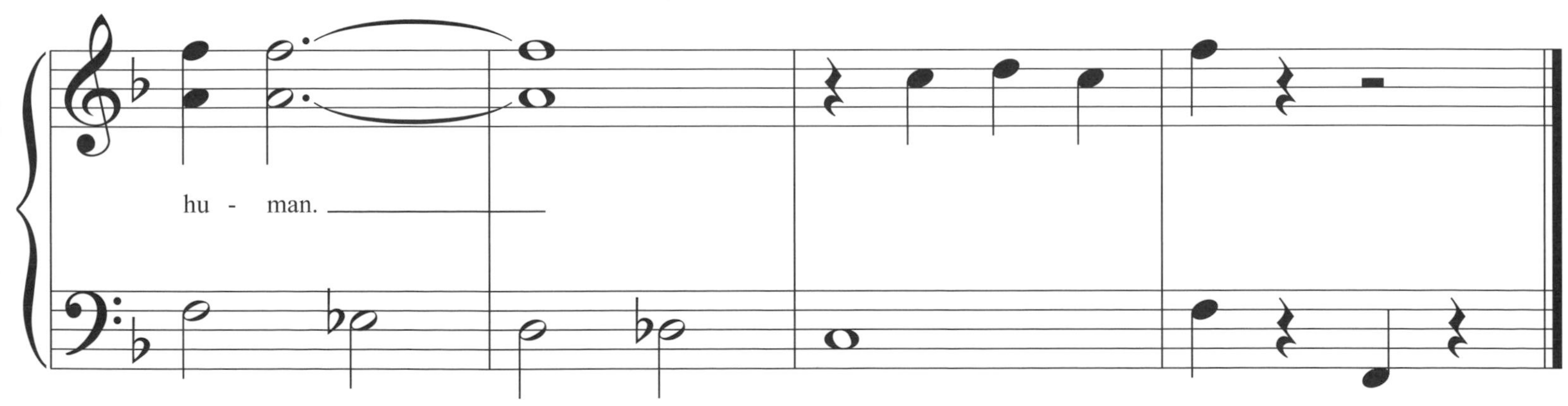
hu - man. ___

SPEECHLESS

from ALADDIN 2019

Music by ALAN MENKEN
Lyrics by BENJ PASEK
and JUSTIN PAUL

3
I won't start to crumble whenever they try to

3
shut me or cut me down.
3
I won't be silenced.

You can't keep me quiet. Won't tremble when you try it. All I know
2

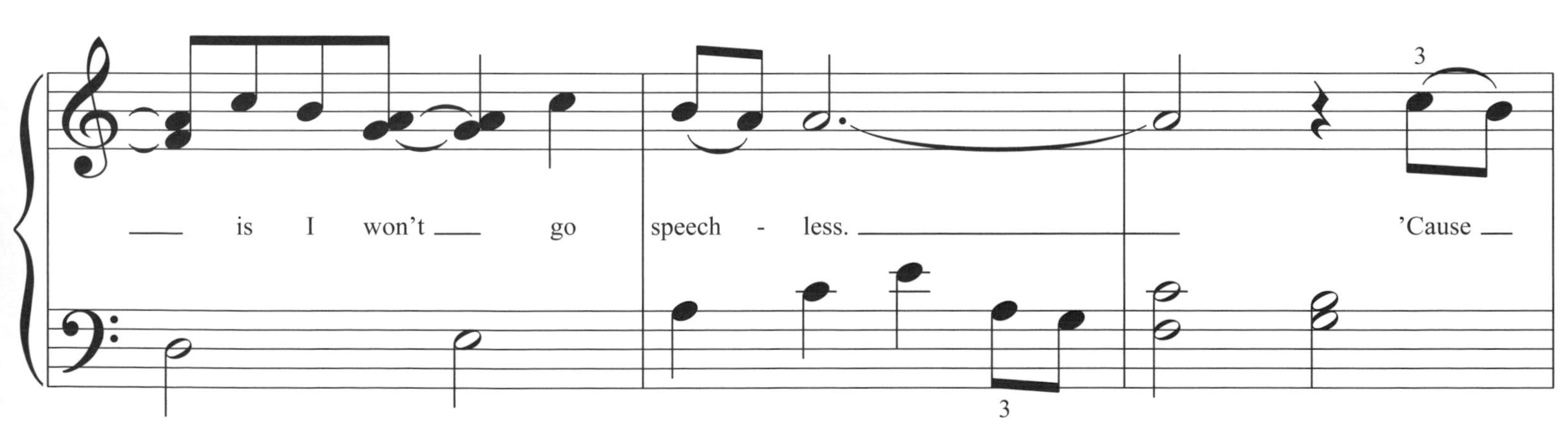
is I won't go speechless.
3
'Cause
3

3
I'll breathe when they try to suf - fo - cate me. Don't you

un - der - es - ti - mate me, 'cause I know that I won't go
2

speech - less.
Writ - ten in stone, ev - 'ry
3

rule, ev - 'ry word, cen - tur - ies old and un - bend - ing.

Stay in your place, __ bet - ter seen ___ and not heard; well, now that sto - ry is
3

2
4
end - ing. 'Cause I, can - not start ___ to

crum - ble. ______ So come on and try, try to shut __
5

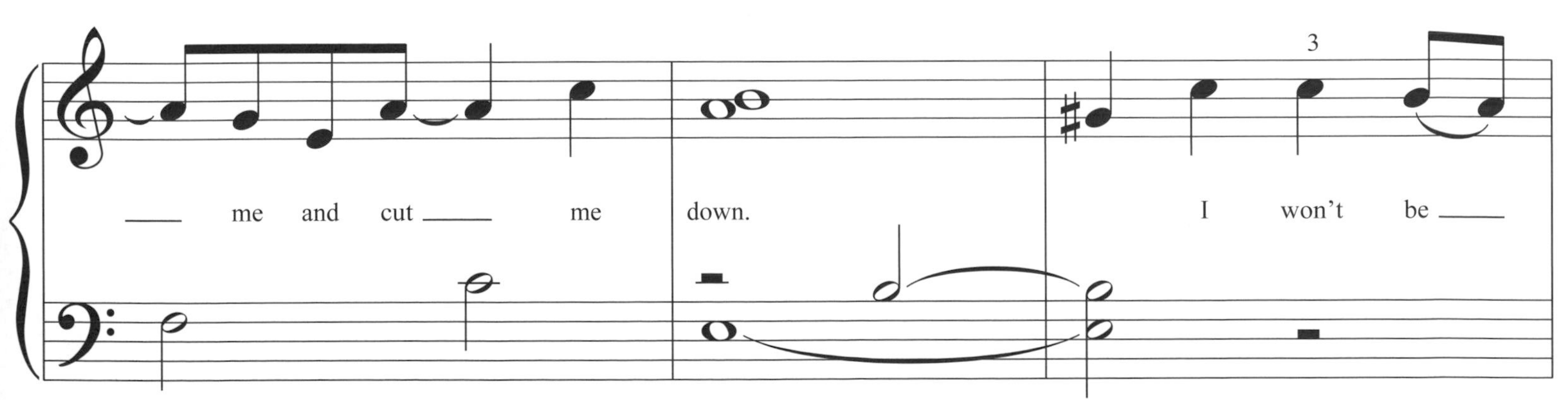
3
___ me and cut ___ me down. I won't be ___

si - lenced. You can't keep me qui - et. Won't

trem - ble when you try it. All I know is I won't go

speech - less. Speech - less. Let the storm in.

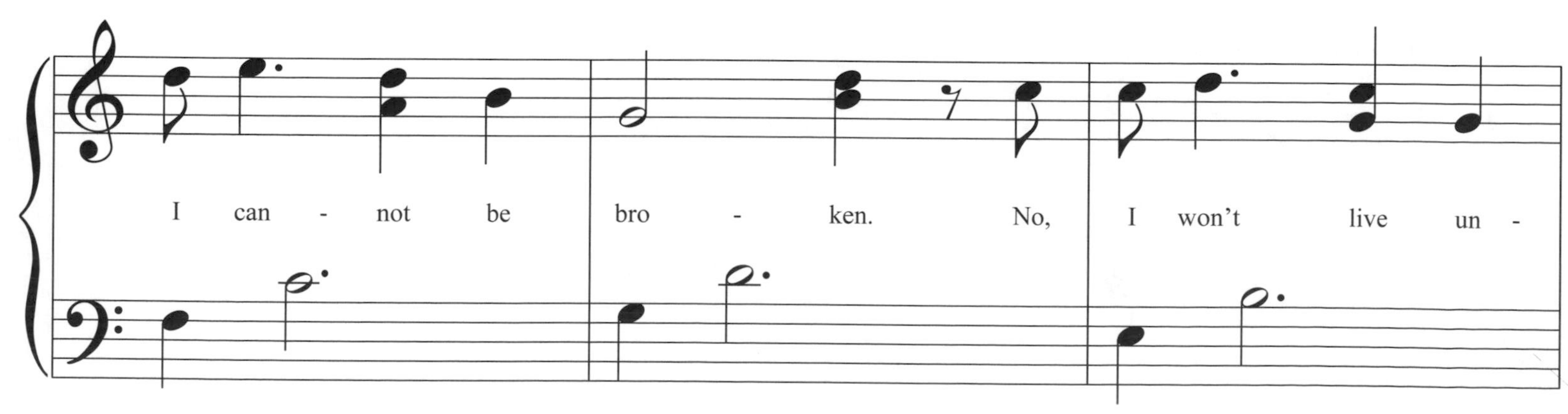
I can - not be bro - ken. No, I won't live un -

spo - ken, 'cause I know that I won't go speech - less.

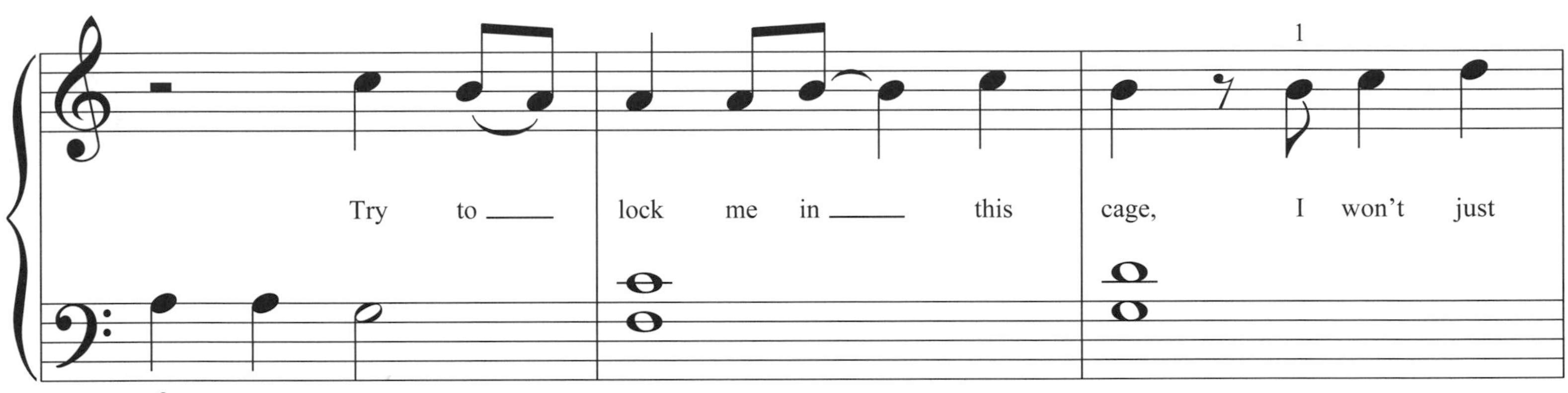
Try to lock me in this cage, I won't just
1
3

lay me down and die. I will take these bro - ken
3
1

wings, and watch me burn a - cross the sky. Hear the

4
ech - o say - ing I won't be si - lenced,
1

though you wan - na see me trem - ble when you

try it. All I know is I won't go speech - less.

3
3
Speech - less. 'Cause I'll breathe when they try to suf - fo -

cate me. Don't you un - der - es - ti - mate me, 'cause I know
that I won't go speech - less. All I know is I won't go
speech - less. Speech - less!
mp

WAKANDA
from BLACK PANTHER

Music by LUDWIG GÖRANSSON

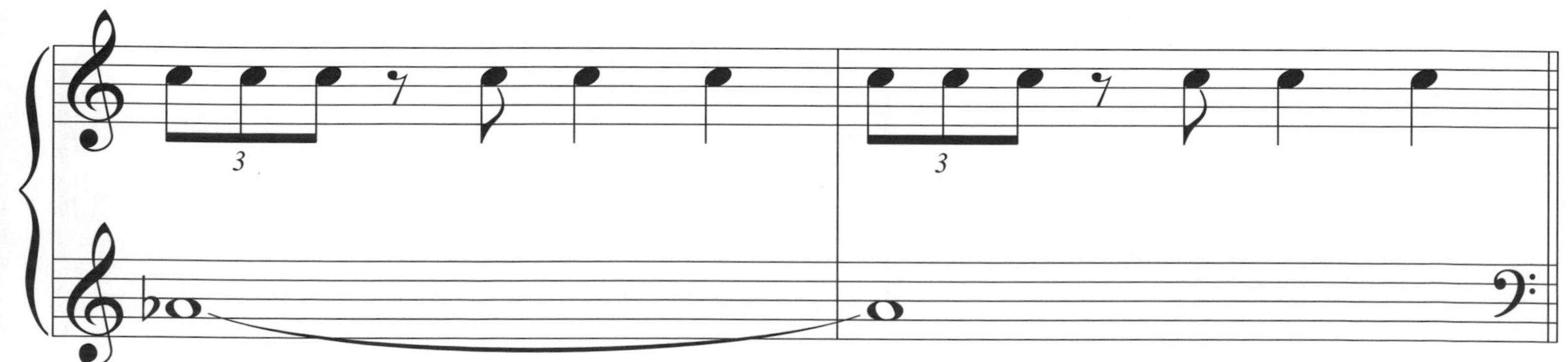

8va
(8va)
(8va)

YOU'VE GOT A FRIEND IN ME

from TOY STORY

Music and Lyrics by
RANDY NEWMAN

Moderately

miles ___ and miles from your nice warm bed, you just re - mem - ber what your
There is - n't an - y - thing I would - n't do for you. If we stick to - geth - er we can
old pal said. Son, you've got a friend in me. Yeah,
see it through, 'cause you've got a friend in me. Yeah,
1.
you've got a friend in me.
2.
you've got a friend in me. ___

3
3
3
Now, some oth - er folks might be a
lit - tle bit smart - er than I am,

3
big - ger and strong - er
too. May - be.

But none of them will
ev - er love ___ you the
way I do, just

4
2
me and you, ___ boy.
And as the years go
by, our

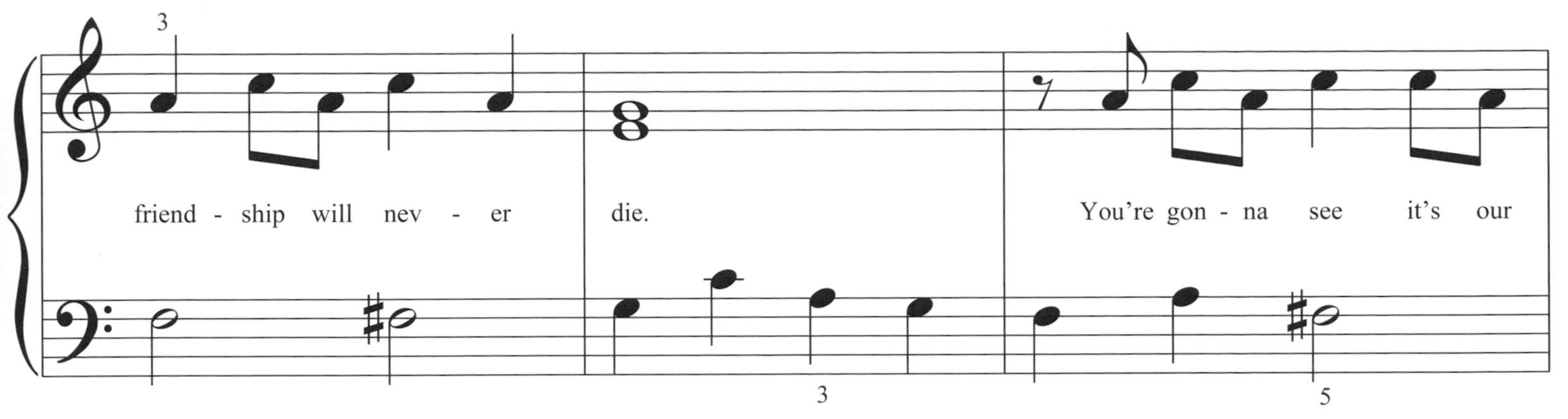
friend - ship will nev - er die. You're gon - na see it's our

des - ti - ny. You've got a friend in me.
rit.
a tempo

You've got a friend in me. You've got a friend in me.

rit.

A WHOLE NEW WORLD

(Aladdin's Theme)
from ALADDIN

Music by ALAN MENKEN
Lyrics by TIM RICE

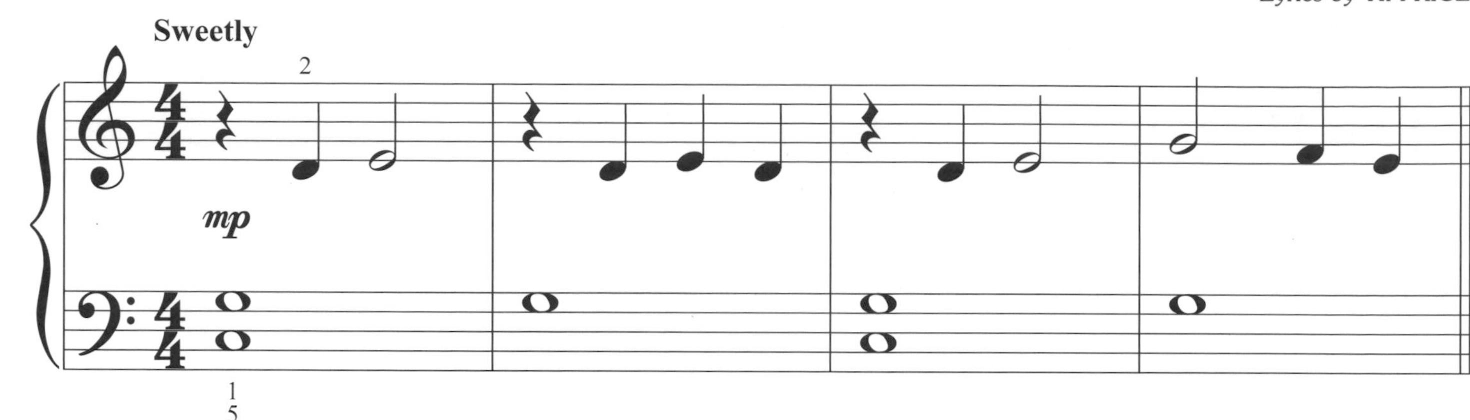

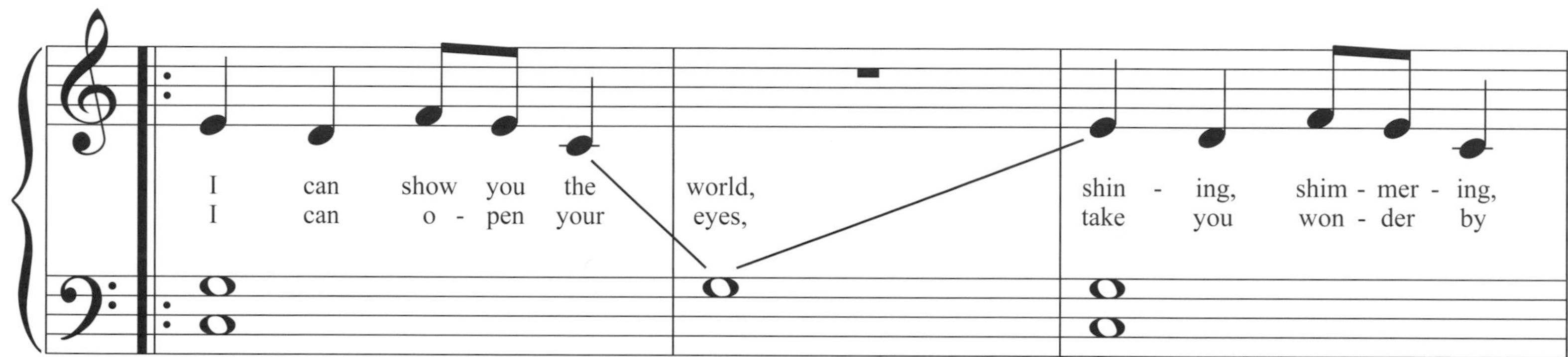

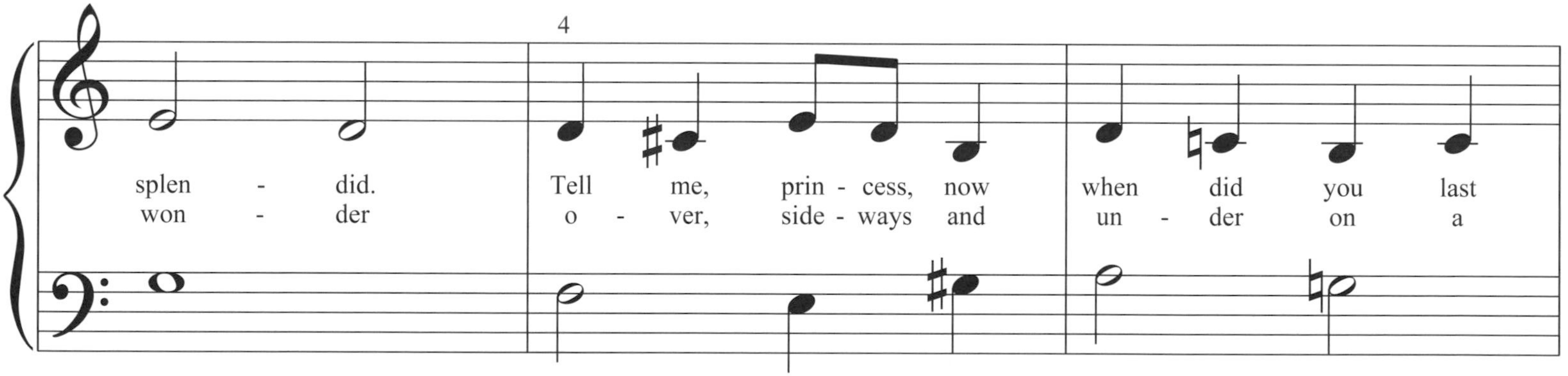

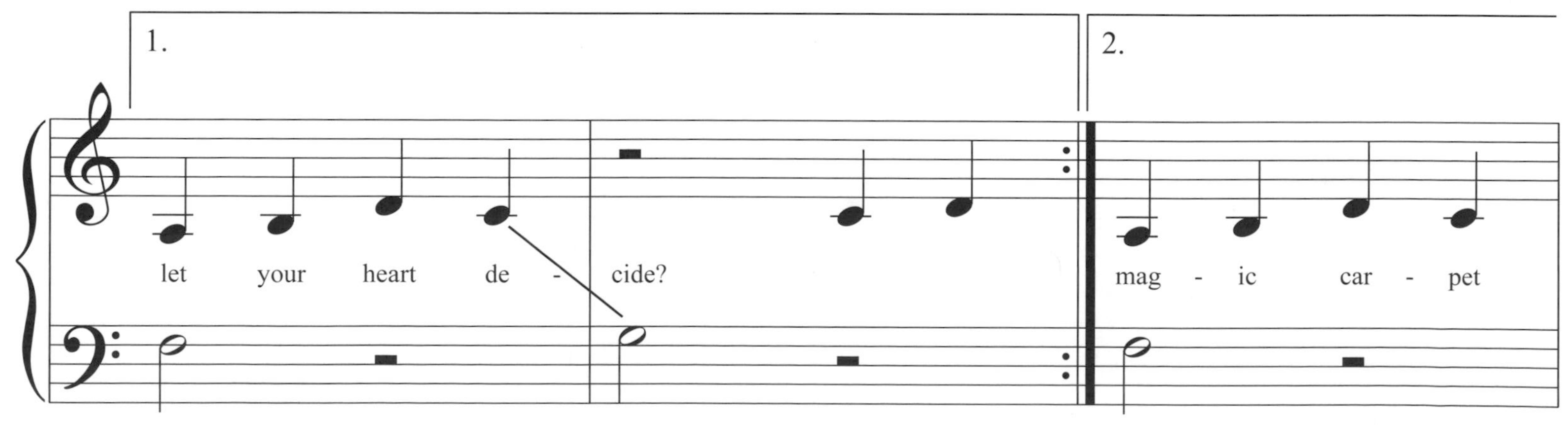

2
ride. A whole new world, a new fan - tas - tic point of view.

No one to tell us no or where to go or

say we're on - ly dream - ing. A whole new world,

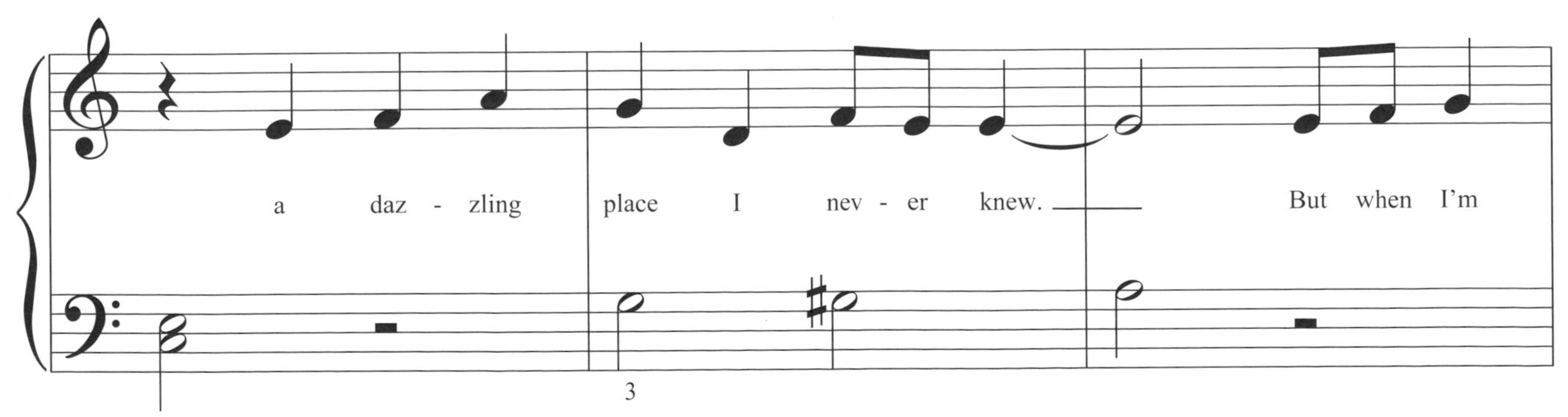
a daz - zling place I nev - er knew. But when I'm
3

1 2
way up here it's crys - tal clear that now I'm in a whole new world with
2

1
3
you.
cresc.
Un - be - liev - a - ble sights,
mf

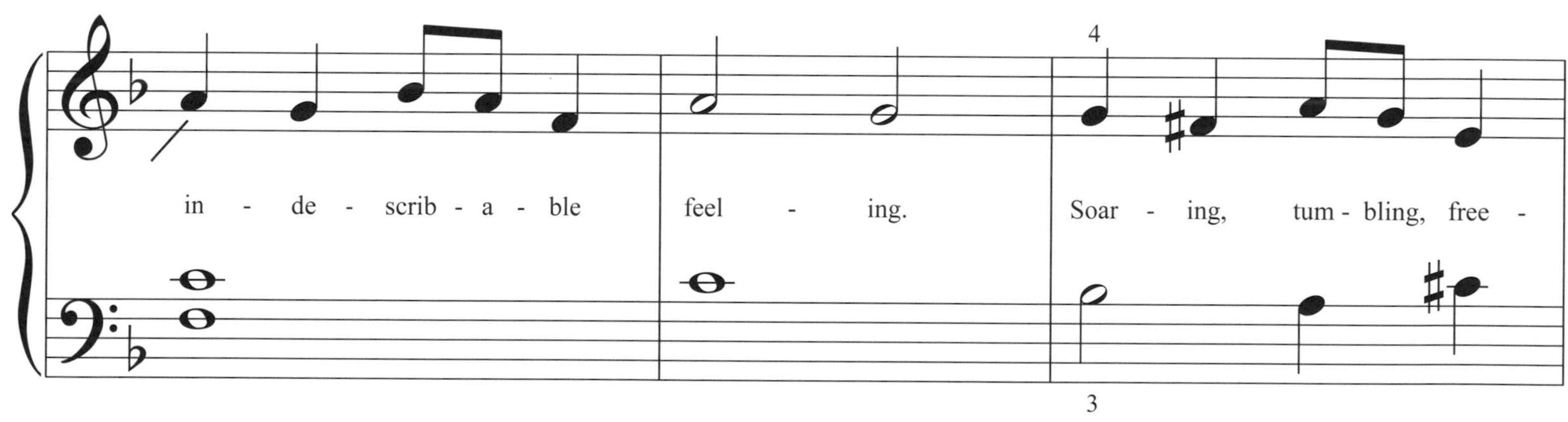
4
in - de - scrib - a - ble feel - ing. Soar - ing, tum - bling, free -
3

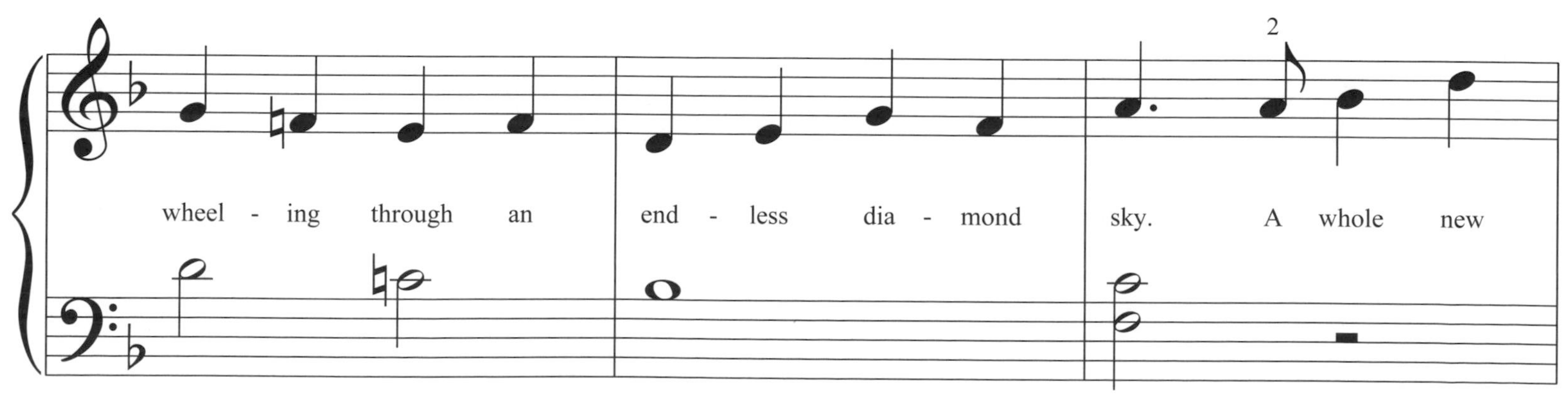
2
wheel - ing through an end - less dia - mond sky. A whole new

world, ___ a hun - dred thou - sand things to see. ___

___ I'm like a shoot - ing star, I've come so far I

can't go back to where I used to be. Ev - 'ry turn a sur -

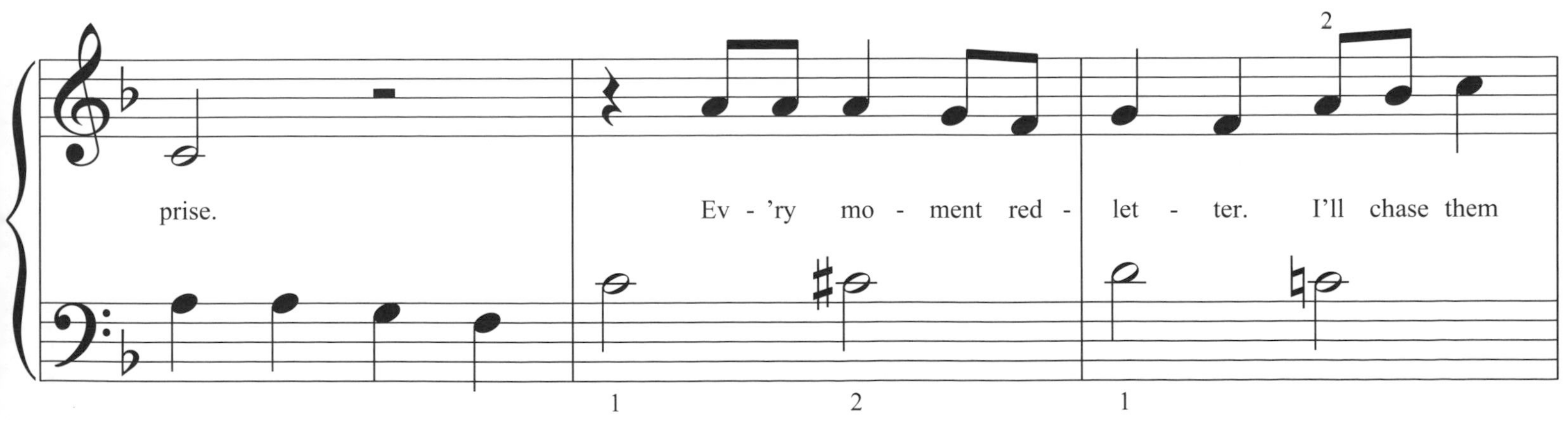
prise. Ev - 'ry mo - ment red - let - ter. I'll chase them

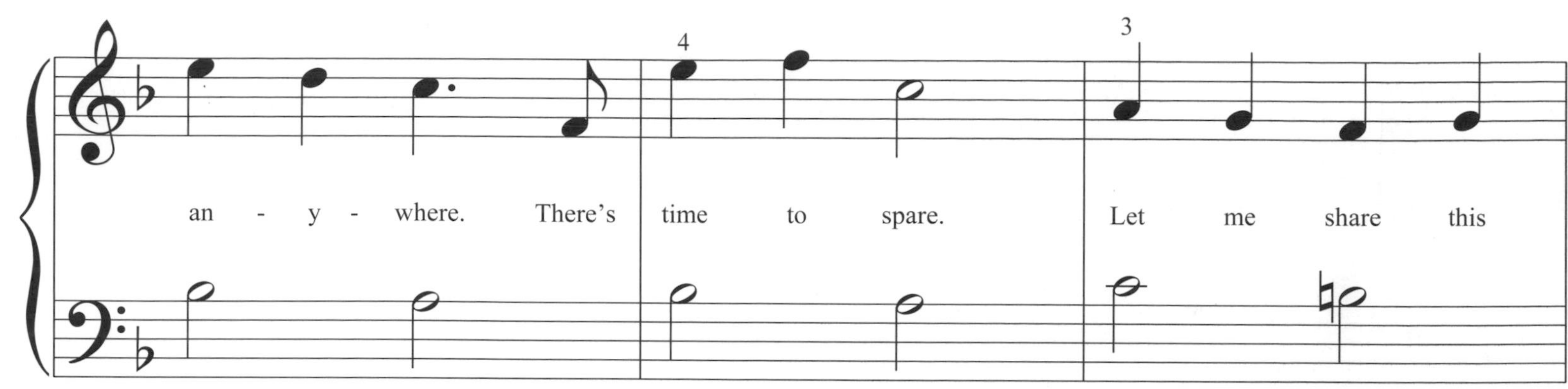
4
3
an - y - where. There's time to spare. Let me share this

2 1
whole new world with you. A whole new world,
dim.
mp

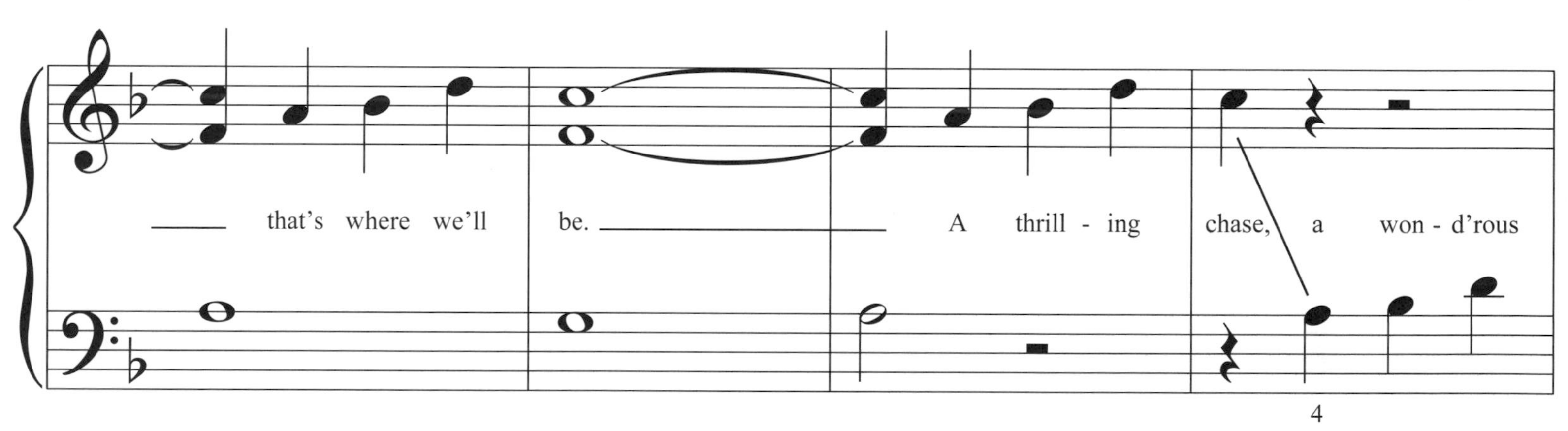
that's where we'll be. A thrill - ing chase, a won - d'rous
4

3
place for you and me.
rit.
1
1
5